The UK Tefal Digital Air Fryer Cookbook 2023

1500 Days Of Healthy And Delicious Tefal Digital Air Fryer Recipes To Satisfy You And Your Family's Taste Buds

Kelly Hays

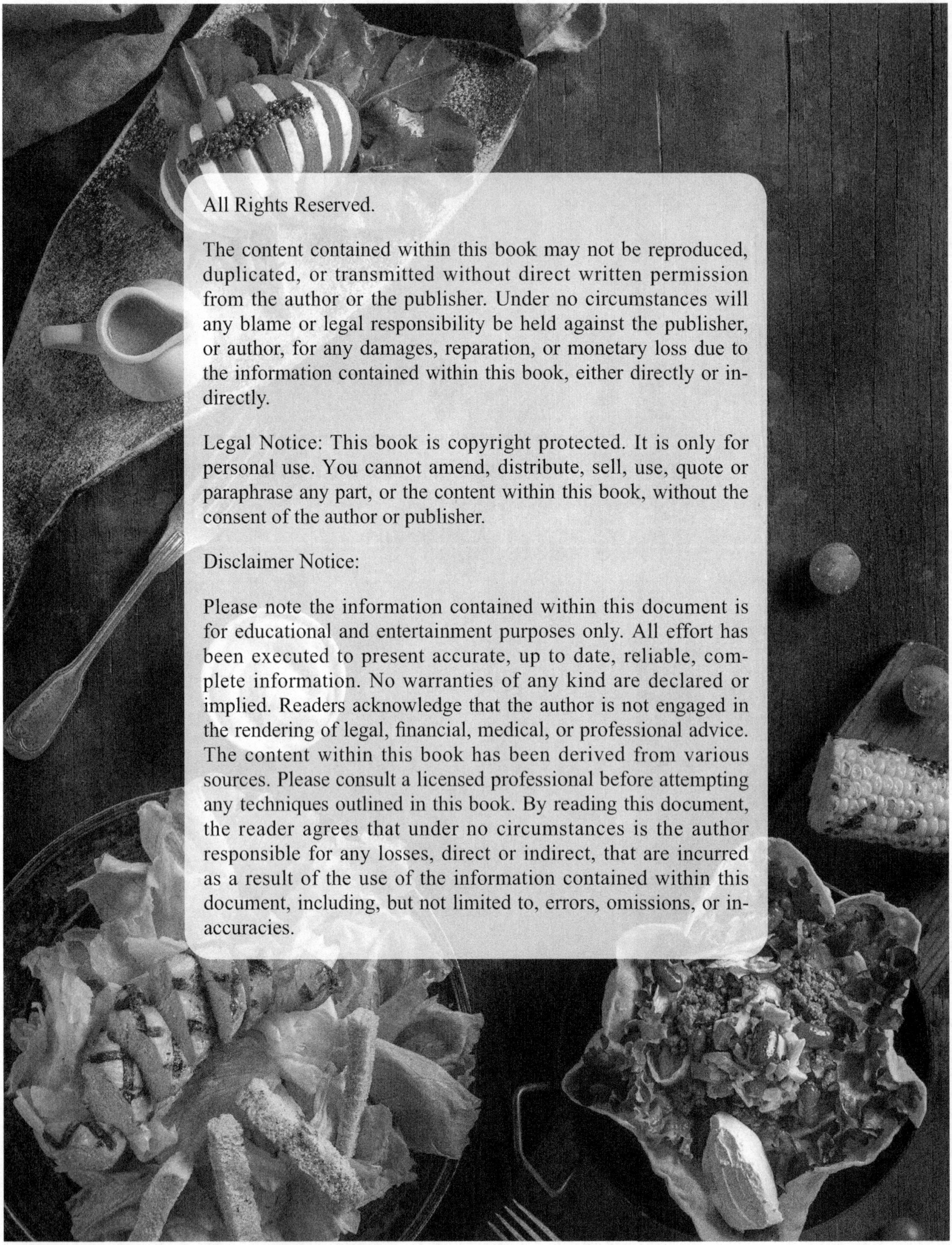

CONTENTS

General Tips for Air-Frying 6

Preparing to air-fry 6
While you are air-frying 6
After you air-fry 7
Re-heating foods in the air-fryer 7
Trouble-shooting 7

Measurement Conversions 8

Bread And Breakfast Recipes 10

Banana Muffins With Chocolate Chips 11
Mini Everything Bagels 11
Garlic Bread Knots 11
Pizza Dough 12
Cinnamon Pumpkin Donuts 12
Scones 12
Mushroom & Cavolo Nero Egg Muffins 13
Goat Cheese, Beet, And Kale Frittata 13
Garlic-cheese Biscuits 13
Morning Chicken Frittata Cups 13
Avocado Toasts With Poached Eggs 14
Vegetarian Quinoa Cups 14
Breakfast Frittata 14
Healthy Granola 14
Oat Bran Muffins 15
Orange Rolls 15
Spring Vegetable Omelet 15
Parsley Egg Scramble With Cottage Cheese 16
Breakfast Chicken Sausages With Apples 16
Southwest Cornbread 16
Canadian Bacon & Cheese Sandwich 16
Roasted Tomato And Cheddar Rolls 17
Whole-grain Cornbread 17
English Scones 17
Seasoned Herbed Sourdough Croutons 18
Huevos Rancheros 18
Cheesy Egg Bites 18
Orange-glazed Cinnamon Rolls 19
Apple & Turkey Breakfast Sausages 19
Aromatic Mushroom Omelet 19

Appetizers And Snacks Recipes 20

Asian-style Shrimp Toast 21
Garlic Wings 21
Jalapeño Poppers 21
Kale Chips 22
Spicy Chicken And Pepper Jack Cheese Bites 22
Parmesan Eggplant Bites 22
Rich Egg-fried Cauliflower Rice 23
Crunchy Spicy Chickpeas 23

Spinach Cups 23
Cheeseburger Slider Pockets 23
Cheddar-pimiento Strips 24
Spanish Fried Baby Squid 24
Garlic-herb Pita Chips 24
Parmesan Pizza Nuggets 25
Fried Gyoza 25
Tasty Roasted Black Olives & Tomatoes 26
“fried” Pickles With Homemade Ranch 26
Tomato & Halloumi Bruschetta 26
Cheese Arancini 26
Middle Eastern Roasted Chickpeas 27
Turkey Bacon Dates 27
Garlic Parmesan Kale Chips 27
Stuffed Prunes In Bacon 28
Crunchy Parmesan Edamame 28
Grilled Ham & Muenster Cheese On Raisin Bread 28
Curried Veggie Samosas 28
Tempura Fried Veggies 29
Cauliflower “tater” Tots 29
Baba Ghanouj 30
Dijon Chicken Wings 30

Desserts And Sweets Recipes 31

Party S´mores 32
Thumbprint Sugar Cookies 32
Easy Churros 32
Strawberry Donuts 33
Chocolate Soufflés 33
Oatmeal Blackberry Crisp 33
Giant Buttery Oatmeal Cookie 34
Caramel Apple Crumble 34
Mini Carrot Cakes 35
Peanut Butter Cup Doughnut Holes 35
Fried Banana S’mores 35
Cheese & Honey Stuffed Figs 36
Fried Pineapple Chunks 36
Cherry Hand Pies 36
Easy Bread Pudding 37
Dark Chocolate Cream Galette 37
Strawberry Donut Bites 37
Coconut Rice Cake 38
Oreo-coated Peanut Butter Cups 38
Healthy Chickpea Cookies 38
Banana Bread Cake 39
Keto Cheesecake Cups 39
Brownies After Dark 39
Pecan-oat Filled Apples 40
Black And Blue Clafoutis 40
Giant Buttery Chocolate Chip Cookie 40
Fried Oreos 41
Cheese Blintzes 41
Lemon Pound Cake Bites 42
Peach Cobbler 42

Beef ,pork & Lamb Recipes 43
Easy Tex-mex Chimichangas 44
Skirt Steak Fajitas 44
Mushroom & Quinoa-stuffed Pork Loins 45
Indian Fry Bread Tacos 45
Beef Short Ribs 45
Perfect Strip Steaks 46
Calzones South Of The Border 46
Lemon-garlic Strip Steak 47
Natchitoches Meat Pies 47
Crispy Ham And Eggs 47
Country-style Pork Ribs 48
Greek Pork Chops 48
Cinnamon-stick Kofta Skewers 48
Calf's Liver 48
Pork Chops With Cereal Crust 49
Mustard-crusted Rib-eye 49
Rib Eye Bites With Mushrooms 49
Zesty London Broil 49
Minted Lamb Chops 50
Blossom Bbq Pork Chops 50
City "chicken" 50
Delicious Juicy Pork Meatballs 51
Rib Eye Cheesesteaks With Fried Onions 51
Kielbasa Chunks With Pineapple & Peppers 51
Bbq Back Ribs 51
Crunchy Fried Pork Loin Chops 52
Glazed Meatloaf 52
French-style Steak Salad 53
Meat Loaves 53
Chipotle Pork Meatballs 53

Poultry Recipes 54
Fiery Chicken Meatballs 55
Buttermilk-fried Drumsticks 55
Indian Chicken Tandoori 55
Lemon Herb Whole Cornish Hen 56
Cajun Fried Chicken 56
Sticky Drumsticks 56
Basic Chicken Breasts 56
Sage & Paprika Turkey Cutlets 56
Jerk Chicken Drumsticks 57
Moroccan-style Chicken Strips 57
Italian Roasted Chicken Thighs 57
Mexican Chicken Roll-ups 58
Cajun Chicken Livers 58
Peachy Chicken Chunks With Cherries 58
Irresistible Cheesy Chicken Sticks 58
Poblano Bake 59
Honey-glazed Cornish Hen 59
Gingery Turkey Meatballs 59
Lemon Sage Roast Chicken 59
Tortilla Crusted Chicken Breast 60
Spinach And Feta Stuffed Chicken Breasts 60
Basic Chicken Breasts 61
Pickle Brined Fried Chicken 61

Turkey Tenderloin With A Lemon Touch ... 61
Za'atar Chicken Drumsticks ... 62
Party Buffalo Chicken Drumettes ... 62
Italian-inspired Chicken Pizzadillas ... 62
Simple Salsa Chicken Thighs ... 62
Farmer´s Fried Chicken ... 63
Cal-mex Turkey Patties ... 63

Fish And Seafood Recipes ... 64

Catalan-style Crab Samfaina ... 65
Blackened Catfish ... 65
Speedy Shrimp Paella ... 65
Old Bay Fish `n´ Chips ... 65
Mexican-style Salmon Stir-fry ... 66
Fried Scallops ... 66
Seared Scallops In Beurre Blanc ... 66
Catfish Nuggets ... 67
Maple Balsamic Glazed Salmon ... 67
Blackened Red Snapper ... 67
Sesame-crusted Tuna Steaks ... 67
Coconut Shrimp With Plum Sauce ... 68
Sardinas Fritas ... 68
Corn & Shrimp Boil ... 68
Shrimp Al Pesto ... 68
Home-style Fish Sticks ... 69
Peppery Tilapia Roulade ... 69
Salmon Croquettes ... 69
Malaysian Shrimp With Sambal Mayo ... 69
Rich Salmon Burgers With Broccoli Slaw ... 70
Garlic And Dill Salmon ... 70
Lime Bay Scallops ... 70
Garlic-butter Lobster Tails ... 70
Fish Goujons With Tartar Sauce ... 71
Asian-style Salmon Fillets ... 71
Filled Mushrooms With Crab & Cheese ... 71
Butternut Squash–wrapped Halibut Fillets ... 71
Parmesan Fish Bites ... 72
Halibut With Coleslaw ... 72
Sea Scallops ... 72

Vegetable Side Dishes Recipes ... 73

Asparagus & Cherry Tomato Roast ... 74
Sweet Potato Curly Fries ... 74
Moroccan-spiced Carrots ... 74
Fried Eggplant Slices ... 74
Simple Baked Potatoes With Dill Yogurt ... 75
Creole Potato Wedges ... 75
Buttery Radish Wedges ... 75
Sweet Potato Fries ... 76
Air-fried Potato Salad ... 76
Garlicky Bell Pepper Mix ... 76
Turkish Mutabal (eggplant Dip) ... 76
Mashed Potato Tots ... 77
Dauphinoise (potatoes Au Gratin) ... 77
Classic Stuffed Shells ... 77
Perfect Asparagus ... 77
Zucchini Fries ... 78

Cheese-rice Stuffed Bell Peppers 78
Sticky Broccoli Florets 78
Buttery Rolls 79
Grilled Lime Scallions 79
Basic Corn On The Cob 79
Southern Okra Chips 80
Roasted Herbed Shiitake Mushrooms 80
Fried Corn On The Cob 80
Tasty Brussels Sprouts With Guanciale 80
Pork Tenderloin Salad 81
Florentine Stuffed Tomatoes 81
Patatas Bravas 81
Crispy, Cheesy Leeks 82
Cauliflower 82

Vegetarians Recipes 83

Sweet Corn Bread 84
Gorgeous Jalapeño Poppers 84
Crispy Avocados With Pico De Gallo 84
Sushi-style Deviled Eggs 84
Veggie Samosas 85
Tomato & Squash Stuffed Mushrooms 85
Bengali Samosa With Mango Chutney 85
Two-cheese Grilled Sandwiches 86
Veggie Burgers 86
Charred Cauliflower Tacos 86
Pizza Margherita With Spinach 86
Curried Potato, Cauliflower And Pea Turnovers 87
Vietnamese Gingered Tofu 87
Breaded Avocado Tacos 88
Lentil Burritos With Cilantro Chutney 88
Quinoa Burgers With Feta Cheese And Dill 88
Vegetable Couscous 89
Tandoori Paneer Naan Pizza 89
Farfalle With White Sauce 90
Fried Rice With Curried Tofu 90
Vegan Buddha Bowls 90
Powerful Jackfruit Fritters 91
Tortilla Pizza Margherita 91
Spicy Sesame Tempeh Slaw With Peanut Dressing 91
Harissa Veggie Fries 92
Kale & Lentils With Crispy Onions 92
Mushroom Lasagna 92
General Tso's Cauliflower 93
Italian-style Fried Cauliflower 93
Garlicky Roasted Mushrooms 93

Appendix : Recipes Index 94

General Tips for Air-Frying

Preparing to air-fry

•Find the right place for your air fryer in your kitchen. Always keep your air fryer on a level, heat-resistant countertop and make sure there are at least five inches of space behind the air fryer where the exhaust vent is located.

•Pre-heat your air fryer before adding your food. This is easy – just turn the air fryer on to the temperature that you need and set the timer for 2 or 3 minutes. When the timer goes off, the air fryer has pre-heated and is ready for food.

•Invest in a kitchen spray bottle. Spraying oil on the food is easier than drizzling or brushing, and allows you to use less oil overall. While you can buy oil sprays in cans, sometimes there are aerosol agents in those cans that can break down the non-stick surface on your air fryer basket. So, if you want to spray foods directly in the basket, invest in a hand-pumped kitchen spray bottle. It will be worth it!

•Get the right accessories. Once you start air frying, you may want to invest in some accessories for your new favorite appliance. Truth is, you may already have some! Any baking dishes or cake pans that are oven-safe should be air fryer-safe as well, as long as they don't come in contact with the heating element. The only stipulation, of course, is that the accessory pan has to be able to fit inside the air fryer basket.

While you are air-frying

•Don't overcrowd the basket. I can't stress this enough. It's tempting to try to cook more at one time, but over-crowding the basket will prevent foods from crisping and browning evenly and take more time over all.

•Flip foods over halfway through the cooking time. Just as you would if you were cooking on a grill or in a skillet, you need to turn foods over so that they brown evenly.

•Open the air fryer as often as you like to check for doneness. This is one of the best parts of air fryers – you can open that drawer as often as you like (within reason) to check to see how the cooking process is coming along. This will not interrupt the timing of most air fryers – the fryer will either continue heating and timing as you pull the basket out, or pick up where it left off when you return the basket to the fryer.

•Shake the basket. Shaking the basket a couple of times during the cooking process will re-distribute the ingredients and help them to brown and crisp more evenly.

•Spray with oil part way through. If you are trying to get the food to brown and crisp more, try spritzing it with oil part way through the cooking process. This will also help the food to brown more evenly.

After you air-fry

•Remove the air fryer basket from the drawer before turning out foods. This is very important and it's a mistake you'll only make once. If you invert the basket while it is still locked into the air fryer drawer, you will end up dumping all the rendered fat or excess grease onto your plate along with the food you just air-fried.

•Clean the drawer as well as the basket after every use. The drawer of the air fryer is very easy to clean, so don't put it off. If you leave it unwashed, you'll run the risk of food contamination and your kitchen won't smell very nice in a day or so!

•Use the air fryer to dry itself. After washing the air fryer basket and drawer, just pop them back into the air fryer and turn it on for 2 or 3 minutes. That dries both parts better than any drying towel.

Re-heating foods in the air-fryer

•There's no hard and fast rule for time and temperature when re-heating leftovers because leftovers vary so significantly. I suggest re-heating in the air fryer at 180°C/350°F and doing so for as long as it takes for the food to be re-heated to a food safety temperature of 75°C/165°F. This is especially important for any potentially hazardous foods like chicken, pork and beef.

Trouble-shooting

•Food is not getting crispy enough. Make sure you are not over-crowding the air fryer basket and make sure you are using a little oil.

•There is white smoke coming from the air fryer. Add some water to the air fryer drawer underneath the basket. The white smoke is probably because grease has drained into the drawer and is burning. Adding water will prevent this.

•There is black smoke coming from the air fryer. Turn the machine off and look up towards the heating element inside the fryer. Some food might have blown up and attached to the heating element, burning and causing the black smoke.

•The air fryer won't turn off. Many air fryers are designed to have a delay in their shutting down process. Once you press the power button off, the fan will continue to blow the hot air out of the unit for about 20 seconds. Don't press the power button again, or you will have just turned the machine back on. Be patient and wait, and the air fryer will turn off.

Measurement Conversions

BASIC KITCHEN CONVERSIONS & EQUIVALENTS

DRY MEASUREMENTS CONVERSION CHART

3 TEASPOONS = 1 TABLESPOON = 1/16 CUP

6 TEASPOONS = 2 TABLESPOONS = 1/8 CUP

12 TEASPOONS = 4 TABLESPOONS = 1/4 CUP

24 TEASPOONS = 8 TABLESPOONS = 1/2 CUP

36 TEASPOONS = 12 TABLESPOONS = 3/4 CUP

48 TEASPOONS = 16 TABLESPOONS = 1 CUP

METRIC TO US COOKING CONVER-SIONS

OVEN TEMPERATURES

120 °C = 250 °F

160 °C = 320 °F

180° C = 350 °F

205 °C = 400 °F

220 °C = 425 °F

LIQUID MEASUREMENTS CONVERSION CHART

8 FLUID OUNCES = 1 CUP = 1/2 PINT = 1/4 QUART

16 FLUID OUNCES = 2 CUPS = 1 PINT = 1/2 QUART

32 FLUID OUNCES = 4 CUPS = 2 PINTS = 1 QUART

= 1/4 GALLON

128 FLUID OUNCES = 16 CUPS = 8 PINTS = 4 QUARTS = 1 GALLON

BAKING IN GRAMS

1 CUP FLOUR = 140 GRAMS

1 CUP SUGAR = 150 GRAMS

1 CUP POWDERED SUGAR = 160 GRAMS

1 CUP HEAVY CREAM = 235 GRAMS

VOLUME

1 MILLILITER = 1/5 TEASPOON

5 ML = 1 TEASPOON

15 ML = 1 TABLESPOON

240 ML = 1 CUP OR 8 FLUID OUNCES

1 LITER = 34 FL. OUNCES

WEIGHT

1 GRAM = .035 OUNCES

100 GRAMS = 3.5 OUNCES

500 GRAMS = 1.1 POUNDS

1 KILOGRAM = 35 OUNCES

US TO METRIC COOKING CONVERSIONS

1/5 TSP = 1 ML

1 TSP = 5 ML

1 TBSP = 15 ML

1 FL OUNCE = 30 ML

1 CUP = 237 ML

1 PINT (2 CUPS) = 473 ML

1 QUART (4 CUPS) = .95 LITER

1 GALLON (16 CUPS) = 3.8 LITERS

1 OZ = 28 GRAMS

1 POUND = 454 GRAMS

BUTTER

1 CUP BUTTER = 2 STICKS = 8 OUNCES = 230 GRAMS = 8 TABLESPOONS

WHAT DOES 1 CUP EQUAL

1 CUP = 8 FLUID OUNCES

1 CUP = 16 TABLESPOONS

1 CUP = 48 TEASPOONS

1 CUP = 1/2 PINT

1 CUP = 1/4 QUART

1 CUP = 1/16 GALLON

1 CUP = 240 ML

BAKING PAN CONVERSIONS

1 CUP ALL-PURPOSE FLOUR = 4.5 OZ

1 CUP ROLLED OATS = 3 OZ 1 LARGE EGG = 1.7 OZ

1 CUP BUTTER = 8 OZ 1 CUP MILK = 8 OZ

1 CUP HEAVY CREAM = 8.4 OZ

1 CUP GRANULATED SUGAR = 7.1 OZ

1 CUP PACKED BROWN SUGAR = 7.75 OZ

1 CUP VEGETABLE OIL = 7.7 OZ

1 CUP UNSIFTED POWDERED SUGAR = 4.4 OZ

BAKING PAN CONVERSIONS

9-INCH ROUND CAKE PAN = 12 CUPS

10-INCH TUBE PAN =16 CUPS

11-INCH BUNDT PAN = 12 CUPS

9-INCH SPRINGFORM PAN = 10 CUPS

9 X 5 INCH LOAF PAN = 8 CUPS

9-INCH SQUARE PAN = 8 CUPS

Bread And Break-fast Recipes

Banana Muffins With Chocolate Chips

Servings: 8 | Cooking Time: 25 Minutes

Ingredients:

- 1 cup flour
- ½ tsp baking soda
- 1/3 cup brown sugar
- ¼ tsp salt
- 1/3 cup mashed banana
- ½ tsp vanilla extract
- 1 egg
- 1 tbsp vegetable oil
- ¼ cup chocolate chips
- 1 tbsp powdered sugar

Directions:

1. Preheat air fryer at 375ºF. Combine dry ingredients in a bowl. In another bowl, mix wet ingredients. Pour wet ingredients into dry ingredients and gently toss to combine. Fold in chocolate chips. Do not overmix.
2. Spoon mixture into 8 greased silicone cupcake liners, place them in the frying basket, and Bake for 6-8 minutes. Let cool onto a cooling rack. Serve right away sprinkled with powdered sugar.

Mini Everything Bagels

Servings: 4 | Cooking Time: 6 Minutes

Ingredients:

- 1 cup all-purpose flour
- 2 teaspoons baking powder
- ½ teaspoon salt
- 1 cup plain Greek yogurt
- 1 egg, whisked
- 1 teaspoon sesame seeds
- 1 teaspoon dehydrated onions
- ½ teaspoon poppy seeds
- ½ teaspoon garlic powder
- ½ teaspoon sea salt flakes

Directions:

1. In a large bowl, mix together the flour, baking powder, and salt. Make a well in the dough and add in the Greek yogurt. Mix with a spoon until a dough forms.
2. Place the dough onto a heavily floured surface and knead for 3 minutes. You may use up to 1 cup of additional flour as you knead the dough, if necessary.
3. Cut the dough into 8 pieces and roll each piece into a 6-inch, snakelike piece. Touch the ends of each piece together so it closes the circle and forms a bagel shape. Brush the tops of the bagels with the whisked egg.
4. In a small bowl, combine the sesame seeds, dehydrated onions, poppy seeds, garlic powder, and sea salt flakes. Sprinkle the seasoning on top of the bagels.
5. Preheat the air fryer to 360°F. Using a bench scraper or flat-edged spatula, carefully place the bagels into the air fryer basket. Spray the bagel tops with cooking spray. Air-fry the bagels for 6 minutes or until golden brown. Allow the bread to cool at least 10 minutes before slicing for serving.

Garlic Bread Knots

Servings: 8 | Cooking Time: 5 Minutes

Ingredients:

- ¼ cup melted butter
- 2 teaspoons garlic powder
- 1 teaspoon dried parsley
- 1 (11-ounce) tube of refrigerated French bread dough

Directions:

1. Mix the melted butter, garlic powder and dried parsley in a small bowl and set it aside.
2. To make smaller knots, cut the long tube of bread dough into 16 slices. If you want to make bigger knots, slice the dough into 8 slices. Shape each slice into a long rope about 6 inches long by rolling it on a flat surface with the palm of your hands. Tie each rope into a knot and place them on a plate.
3. Preheat the air fryer to 350°F.
4. Transfer half of the bread knots into the air fryer basket, leaving space in between each knot. Brush each knot with the butter mixture using a pastry brush.
5. Air-fry for 5 minutes. Remove the baked knots and brush a little more of the garlic butter mixture on each. Repeat with the remaining bread knots and serve warm.

Pizza Dough

Servings: 3 | Cooking Time: 10 Minutes

Ingredients:

- 4 cups bread flour, pizza ("00") flour or all-purpose flour
- 1 teaspoon active dry yeast
- 2 teaspoons sugar
- 2 teaspoons salt
- 1½ cups water
- 1 tablespoon olive oil

Directions:

1. Combine the flour, yeast, sugar and salt in the bowl of a stand mixer. Add the olive oil to the flour mixture and start to mix using the dough hook attachment. As you're mixing, add 1¼ cups of the water, mixing until the dough comes together. Continue to knead the dough with the dough hook for another 10 minutes, adding enough water to the dough to get it to the right consistency.
2. Transfer the dough to a floured counter and divide it into 3 equal portions. Roll each portion into a ball. Lightly coat each dough ball with oil and transfer to the refrigerator, covered with plastic wrap. You can place them all on a baking sheet, or place each dough ball into its own oiled zipper sealable plastic bag or container. (You can freeze the dough balls at this stage, removing as much air as possible from the oiled bag.) Keep in the refrigerator for at least one day, or as long as five days.
3. When you're ready to use the dough, remove your dough from the refrigerator at least 1 hour prior to baking and let it sit on the counter, covered gently with plastic wrap.

Cinnamon Pumpkin Donuts

Servings: 6 | Cooking Time: 30 Minutes

Ingredients:

- 1/3 cup canned pumpkin purée
- 1 cup flour
- 3 tbsp brown sugar
- ½ tsp ground cinnamon
- 1/8 tsp ground nutmeg
- 1 tsp baking powder
- 3 tbsp milk
- 2 tbsp butter, melted
- 1 large egg
- 3 tbsp powdered sugar

Directions:

1. Combine the flour, brown sugar, cinnamon, nutmeg, and baking powder in a bowl. Whisk the pumpkin, milk, butter, and egg white in another bowl. Pour the pumpkin mixture over the dry ingredients and stir. Add more milk or flour if necessary to make a soft dough. Cover your hands in flour, make 12 pieces from the dough, and form them into balls. Measure the frying basket, then cut foil or parchment paper about an inch smaller than the measurement. Poke holes in it and put it in the basket.
2. Preheat air fryer to 360°F. Set the donut holes in the basket and Air Fry for 5-7 minutes. Allow the donuts to chill for 5 minutes, then roll in powdered sugar. Serve.

Scones

Servings: 9 | Cooking Time: 8 Minutes Per Batch

Ingredients:

- 2 cups self-rising flour, plus ¼ cup for kneading
- ⅓ cup granulated sugar
- ¼ cup butter, cold
- 1 cup milk

Directions:

1. Preheat air fryer at 360°F.
2. In large bowl, stir together flour and sugar.
3. Cut cold butter into tiny cubes, and stir into flour mixture with fork.
4. Stir in milk until soft dough forms.
5. Sprinkle ¼ cup of flour onto wax paper and place dough on top. Knead lightly by folding and turning the dough about 6 to 8 times.
6. Pat dough into a 6 x 6-inch square.
7. Cut into 9 equal squares.
8. Place all squares in air fryer basket or as many as will fit in a single layer, close together but not touching.
9. Cook at 360°F for 8minutes. When done, scones will be lightly browned on top and will spring back when pressed gently with a dull knife.
10. Repeat steps 8 and 9 to cook remaining scones.

Mushroom & Cavolo Nero Egg Muffins

Servings: 6 | Cooking Time: 20 Minutes

Ingredients:

- 8 oz baby Bella mushrooms, sliced
- 6 eggs, beaten
- 1 garlic clove, minced
- Salt and pepper to taste
- ½ tsp chili powder
- 1 cup cavolo nero
- 2 scallions, diced

Directions:

1. Preheat air fryer to 320°F. Place the eggs, garlic, salt, pepper, and chili powder in a bowl and beat until well combined. Fold in the mushrooms, cavolo nero, and scallions. Divide the mixture between greased muffin cups. Place into the air fryer and Bake for 12-15 minutes, or until the eggs are set. Cool for 5 minutes. Enjoy!

Goat Cheese, Beet, And Kale Frittata

Servings: 6 | Cooking Time: 20 Minutes

Ingredients:

- 6 large eggs
- ½ teaspoon garlic powder
- ¼ teaspoon black pepper
- ¼ teaspoon salt
- 1 cup chopped kale
- 1 cup cooked and chopped red beets
- ⅓ cup crumbled goat cheese

Directions:

1. Preheat the air fryer to 320°F.
2. In a medium bowl, whisk the eggs with the garlic powder, pepper, and salt. Mix in the kale, beets, and goat cheese.
3. Spray an oven-safe 7-inch springform pan with cooking spray. Pour the egg mixture into the pan and place it in the air fryer basket.
4. Cook for 20 minutes, or until the internal temperature reaches 145°F.
5. When the frittata is cooked, let it set for 5 minutes before removing from the pan.
6. Slice and serve immediately.

Garlic-cheese Biscuits

Servings: 8 | Cooking Time: 8 Minutes

Ingredients:

- 1 cup self-rising flour
- 1 teaspoon garlic powder
- 2 tablespoons butter, diced
- 2 ounces sharp Cheddar cheese, grated
- ½ cup milk
- cooking spray

Directions:

1. Preheat air fryer to 330°F.
2. Combine flour and garlic in a medium bowl and stir together.
3. Using a pastry blender or knives, cut butter into dry ingredients.
4. Stir in cheese.
5. Add milk and stir until stiff dough forms.
6. If dough is too sticky to handle, stir in 1 or 2 more tablespoons of self-rising flour before shaping. Biscuits should be firm enough to hold their shape. Otherwise, they'll stick to the air fryer basket.
7. Divide dough into 8 portions and shape into 2-inch biscuits about ¾-inch thick.
8. Spray air fryer basket with nonstick cooking spray.
9. Place all 8 biscuits in basket and cook at 330°F for 8 minutes.

Morning Chicken Frittata Cups

Servings:6 | Cooking Time: 30 Minutes

Ingredients:

- ¼ cup shredded cooked chicken breasts
- 3 eggs
- 2 tbsp heavy cream
- 4 tsp Tabasco sauce
- ¼ cup grated Asiago cheese
- 2 tbsp chives, chopped

Directions:

1. Preheat air fryer to 350ºF. Beat all ingredients in a bowl. Divide the egg mixture between greased 6 muffin cups and place them in the frying basket. Bake for 8-10 minutes until set. Let cool slightly before serving. Enjoy!

Avocado Toasts With Poached Eggs

Servings: 4 | Cooking Time: 15 Minutes

Ingredients:

- 4 eggs
- Salt and pepper to taste
- 4 bread pieces, toasted
- 1 pitted avocado, sliced
- ½ tsp chili powder
- ½ tsp dried rosemary

Directions:

1. Preheat air fryer to 320°F. Crack 1 egg into each greased ramekin and season with salt and black pepper. Place the ramekins into the air frying basket. Bake for 6-8 minutes.
2. Scoop the flesh of the avocado into a small bowl. Season with salt, black pepper, chili powderp and rosemary. Using a fork, smash the avocado lightly. Spread the smashed avocado evenly over toasted bread slices. Remove the eggs from the air fryer and gently spoon one onto each slice of avocado toast. Serve and enjoy!

Vegetarian Quinoa Cups

Servings: 6 | Cooking Time: 25 Minutes

Ingredients:

- 1 carrot, chopped
- 1 zucchini, chopped
- 4 asparagus, chopped
- ¾ cup quinoa flour
- 2 tbsp lemon juice
- ¼ cup nutritional yeast
- ¼ tsp garlic powder
- Salt and pepper to taste

Directions:

1. Preheat air fryer to 340°F. Combine the vegetables, quinoa flour, water, lemon juice, nutritional yeast, garlic powder, salt, and pepper in a medium bowl, and mix well.Divide the mixture between 6 cupcake molds. Place the filled molds into the air fryer and Bake for 20 minutes, or until the tops are lightly browned and a toothpick inserted into the center comes out clean. Serve cooled.

Breakfast Frittata

Servings:2 | Cooking Time: 25 Minutes

Ingredients:

- 4 cooked pancetta slices, chopped
- 5 eggs
- Salt and pepper to taste
- ½ leek, thinly sliced
- ½ cup grated cheddar cheese
- 1 tomato, sliced
- 1 cup iceberg lettuce, torn
- 2 tbsp milk

Directions:

1. Preheat air fryer to 320ºF. Beat the eggs, milk, salt, and pepper in a bowl. Mix in pancetta and cheddar. Transfer to a greased with olive oil baking pan. Top with tomato slices and leek and place it in the frying basket. Bake for 14 minutes. Let cool for 5 minutes. Serve with lettuce.

Healthy Granola

Servings: 4 | Cooking Time: 10 Minutes

Ingredients:

- ¼ cup chocolate hazelnut spread
- 1 cup chopped pecans
- 1 cup quick-cooking oats
- 1 tbsp chia seeds
- 1 tbsp flaxseed
- 1 tbsp sesame seeds
- 1 cup coconut shreds
- ¼ cup maple syrup
- 1 tbsp light brown sugar
- ½ tsp vanilla extract
- ¼ cup hazelnut flour
- 2 tbsp cocoa powder
- Salt to taste

Directions:

1. Preheat air fryer at 350ºF. Combine the pecans, oats, chia seeds, flaxseed, sesame seeds, coconut shreds, chocolate hazelnut spread, maple syrup, sugar, vanilla extract, hazelnut flour, cocoa powder, and salt in a bowl. Press mixture into a greased cake pan. Place cake pan in the frying basket and Bake for 5 minutes, stirring once. Let cool completely before crumbling. Store it into an airtight container up to 5 days.

Oat Bran Muffins

Servings: 8 | Cooking Time: 12 Minutes

Ingredients:

- ⅔ cup oat bran
- ½ cup flour
- ¼ cup brown sugar
- 1 teaspoon baking powder
- ½ teaspoon baking soda
- ⅛ teaspoon salt
- ½ cup buttermilk
- 1 egg
- 2 tablespoons canola oil
- ½ cup chopped dates, raisins, or dried cranberries
- 24 paper muffin cups
- cooking spray

Directions:

1. Preheat air fryer to 330°F.
2. In a large bowl, combine the oat bran, flour, brown sugar, baking powder, baking soda, and salt.
3. In a small bowl, beat together the buttermilk, egg, and oil.
4. Pour buttermilk mixture into bowl with dry ingredients and stir just until moistened. Do not beat.
5. Gently stir in dried fruit.
6. Use triple baking cups to help muffins hold shape during baking. Spray them with cooking spray, place 4 sets of cups in air fryer basket at a time, and fill each one ¾ full of batter.
7. Cook for 12minutes, until top springs back when lightly touched and toothpick inserted in center comes out clean.
8. Repeat for remaining muffins.

Orange Rolls

Servings: 8 | Cooking Time: 10 Minutes

Ingredients:

- parchment paper
- 3 ounces low-fat cream cheese
- 1 tablespoon low-fat sour cream or plain yogurt (not Greek yogurt)
- 2 teaspoons sugar
- ¼ teaspoon pure vanilla extract
- ¼ teaspoon orange extract
- 1 can (8 count) organic crescent roll dough
- ¼ cup chopped walnuts
- ¼ cup dried cranberries
- ¼ cup shredded, sweetened coconut
- butter-flavored cooking spray
- Orange Glaze
- ½ cup powdered sugar
- 1 tablespoon orange juice
- ¼ teaspoon orange extract
- dash of salt

Directions:

1. Cut a circular piece of parchment paper slightly smaller than the bottom of your air fryer basket. Set aside.
2. In a small bowl, combine the cream cheese, sour cream or yogurt, sugar, and vanilla and orange extracts. Stir until smooth.
3. Preheat air fryer to 300°F.
4. Separate crescent roll dough into 8 triangles and divide cream cheese mixture among them. Starting at wide end, spread cheese mixture to within 1 inch of point.
5. Sprinkle nuts and cranberries evenly over cheese mixture.
6. Starting at wide end, roll up triangles, then sprinkle with coconut, pressing in lightly to make it stick. Spray tops of rolls with butter-flavored cooking spray.
7. Place parchment paper in air fryer basket, and place 4 rolls on top, spaced evenly.
8. Cook for 10minutes, until rolls are golden brown and cooked through.
9. Repeat steps 7 and 8 to cook remaining 4 rolls. You should be able to use the same piece of parchment paper twice.
10. In a small bowl, stir together ingredients for glaze and drizzle over warm rolls.

Spring Vegetable Omelet

Servings: 4 | Cooking Time: 20 Minutes

Ingredients:

- ¼ cup chopped broccoli, lightly steamed
- ½ cup grated cheddar cheese
- 6 eggs
- ¼ cup steamed kale
- 1 green onion, chopped
- Salt and pepper to taste

Directions:

1. Preheat air fryer to 360°F. In a bowl, beat the eggs. Stir in kale, broccoli, green onion, and cheddar cheese. Transfer the mixture to a greased baking dish and Bake in the fryer for 15 minutes until golden and crisp. Season to taste and serve immediately.

Parsley Egg Scramble With Cottage Cheese

Servings:2 | Cooking Time: 15 Minutes

Ingredients:

- 1 tbsp cottage cheese, crumbled
- 4 eggs
- Salt and pepper to taste
- 2 tsp heavy cream
- 1 tbsp chopped parsley

Directions:

1. Preheat air fryer to 400ºF. Grease a baking pan with olive oil. Beat the eggs, salt, and pepper in a bowl. Pour it into the pan, place the pan in the frying basket, and Air Fry for 5 minutes. Using a silicone spatula, stir in heavy cream, cottage cheese, and half of parsley and Air Fry for another 2 minutes. Scatter with parsley to serve.

Breakfast Chicken Sausages With Apples

Servings: 6 | Cooking Time: 20 Minutes

Ingredients:

- 1 lb ground chicken
- 1 cup diced apples
- 1 garlic clove, minced
- Salt and pepper to taste
- ½ tsp dried sage
- ½ tsp ginger powder
- ½ tsp ground nutmeg
- ¼ tsp cayenne pepper
- ¼ tsp fennel seed
- 1 tsp chopped onion
- ½ tsp brown sugar

Directions:

1. Preheat air fryer to 350°F. Combine all of the ingredients in a large bowl until well combined. Shape into thick patties. Transfer patties to the parchment-lined frying basket and Air Fry for 3 minutes. Flip the patties and Air Fry for another 3-4 minutes. Serve hot.

Southwest Cornbread

Servings: 6 | Cooking Time: 18 Minutes

Ingredients:

- cooking spray
- ½ cup yellow cornmeal
- ½ cup flour
- 2 teaspoons baking powder
- ½ teaspoon salt
- ½ cup frozen corn kernels, thawed and drained
- ¼ cup finely chopped onion
- 1 or 2 small jalapeño peppers, seeded and chopped
- 1 egg
- ½ cup milk
- 2 tablespoons melted butter
- 2 ounces sharp Cheddar cheese, grated

Directions:

1. Preheat air fryer to 360°F.
2. Spray air fryer baking pan with nonstick cooking spray.
3. In a medium bowl, stir together the cornmeal, flour, baking powder, and salt.
4. Stir in the corn, onion, and peppers.
5. In a small bowl, beat together the egg, milk, and butter. Stir into dry ingredients until well combined.
6. Spoon half the batter into prepared baking pan, spreading to edges. Top with grated cheese. Spoon remaining batter on top of cheese and gently spread to edges of pan so it completely covers the cheese.
7. Cook at 360°F for 18 minutes, until cornbread is done and top is crispy brown.

Canadian Bacon & Cheese Sandwich

Servings: 1 | Cooking Time: 30 Minutes

Ingredients:

- 1 English muffin, halved
- 1 egg
- 1 Canadian bacon slice
- 1 slice provolone cheese

Directions:

1. Preheat air fryer to 350°F. Put the muffin, crusty side up, in the frying basket. Place a slice of bacon next to the muffins and Bake for 5 minutes. Flip the bacon and muffins, and lay a slice of provolone cheese on top of the muffins. Beat the egg in a small heatproof bowl.
2. Add the bowl in the frying basket next to the bacon and muffins and Bake for 15 minutes, or until the

cheese melts, bacon is crispy and eggs set. Remove the muffin to a plate, layer a slice of bacon, then the egg and top with the second toasted muffin.

Roasted Tomato And Cheddar Rolls

Servings: 12 | Cooking Time: 55 Minutes

Ingredients:

- 4 Roma tomatoes
- ½ clove garlic, minced
- 1 tablespoon olive oil
- ¼ teaspoon dried thyme
- salt and freshly ground black pepper
- 4 cups all-purpose flour
- 1 teaspoon active dry yeast
- 2 teaspoons sugar
- 2 teaspoons salt
- 1 tablespoon olive oil
- 1 cup grated Cheddar cheese, plus more for sprinkling at the end
- 1½ cups water

Directions:

1. Cut the Roma tomatoes in half, remove the seeds with your fingers and transfer to a bowl. Add the garlic, olive oil, dried thyme, salt and freshly ground black pepper and toss well.
2. Preheat the air fryer to 390°F.
3. Place the tomatoes, cut side up in the air fryer basket and air-fry for 10 minutes. The tomatoes should just start to brown. Shake the basket to redistribute the tomatoes, and air-fry for another 5 to 10 minutes at 330°F until the tomatoes are no longer juicy. Let the tomatoes cool and then rough chop them.
4. Combine the flour, yeast, sugar and salt in the bowl of a stand mixer. Add the olive oil, chopped roasted tomatoes and Cheddar cheese to the flour mixture and start to mix using the dough hook attachment. As you're mixing, add 1¼ cups of the water, mixing until the dough comes together. Continue to knead the dough with the dough hook for another 10 minutes, adding enough water to the dough to get it to the right consistency.
5. Transfer the dough to an oiled bowl, cover with a clean kitchen towel and let it rest and rise until it has doubled in volume – about 1 to 2 hours. Then, divide the dough into 12 equal portions. Roll each portion of dough into a ball. Lightly coat each dough ball with oil and let the dough balls rest and rise a second time, covered lightly with plastic wrap for 45 minutes. (Alternately, you can place the rolls in the refrigerator overnight and take them out 2 hours before you bake them.)
6. Preheat the air fryer to 360°F.
7. Spray the dough balls and the air fryer basket with a little olive oil. Place three rolls at a time in the basket and bake for 10 minutes. Add a little grated Cheddar cheese on top of the rolls for the last 2 minutes of air frying for an attractive finish.

Whole-grain Cornbread

Servings: 6 | Cooking Time: 25 Minutes

Ingredients:

- 1 cup stoneground cornmeal
- ½ cup brown rice flour
- 1 teaspoon sugar
- 2 teaspoons baking powder
- ¼ teaspoon salt
- 1 cup milk
- 2 tablespoons oil
- 2 eggs
- cooking spray

Directions:

1. Preheat the air fryer to 360°F.
2. In a medium mixing bowl, mix cornmeal, brown rice flour, sugar, baking powder, and salt together.
3. Add the remaining ingredients and beat with a spoon until batter is smooth.
4. Spray air fryer baking pan with nonstick cooking spray and add the cornbread batter.
5. Bake at 360°F for 25 minutes, until center is done.

English Scones

Servings: 8 | Cooking Time: 8 Minutes

Ingredients:

- 2 cups all-purpose flour
- 1 tablespoon baking powder
- ½ teaspoon salt
- 2 tablespoons sugar
- ¼ cup unsalted butter
- ⅔ cup plus 1 tablespoon whole milk, divided

Directions:

1. Preheat the air fryer to 380°F.
2. In a large bowl, whisk together the flour, baking powder, salt, and sugar. Using a pastry blender or your fingers, cut in the butter until pea-size crumbles appear. Make a well in the center and pour in ⅔ cup

of the milk. Quickly mix the batter until a ball forms. Knead the dough 3 times.

3. Place the dough onto a floured surface and, using your hands or a rolling pin, flatten the dough until it's ¾ inch thick. Using a biscuit cutter or drinking glass, cut out 10 circles, reforming the dough and flattening as needed to use up the batter.

4. Brush the tops lightly with the remaining 1 tablespoon of milk.

5. Place the scones into the air fryer basket. Cook for 8 minutes or until golden brown and cooked in the center.

Seasoned Herbed Sourdough Croutons

Servings: 4 | Cooking Time: 7 Minutes

Ingredients:

- 4 cups cubed sourdough bread, 1-inch cubes (about 8 ounces)
- 1 tablespoon olive oil
- 1 teaspoon fresh thyme leaves
- ¼ – ½ teaspoon salt
- freshly ground black pepper

Directions:

1. Combine all ingredients in a bowl and taste to make sure it is seasoned to your liking.
2. Preheat the air fryer to 400°F.
3. Toss the bread cubes into the air fryer and air-fry for 7 minutes, shaking the basket once or twice while they cook.
4. Serve warm or store in an airtight container.

Huevos Rancheros

Servings: 4 | Cooking Time: 45 Minutes + Cooling Time

Ingredients:

- 1 tbsp olive oil
- 20 cherry tomatoes, halved
- 2 chopped plum tomatoes
- ¼ cup tomato sauce
- 2 scallions, sliced
- 2 garlic cloves, minced
- 1 tsp honey
- ½ tsp salt
- ⅛ tsp cayenne pepper
- ¼ tsp grated nutmeg
- ¼ tsp paprika
- 4 eggs

Directions:

1. Preheat the air fryer to 370°F. Combine the olive oil, cherry tomatoes, plum tomatoes, tomato sauce, scallions, garlic, nutmeg, honey, salt, paprika and cayenne in a 7-inch springform pan that has been wrapped in foil to prevent leaks. Put the pan in the frying basket and
2. Bake the mix for 15-20 minutes, stirring twice until the tomatoes are soft. Mash some of the tomatoes in the pan with a fork, then stir them into the sauce. Also, break the eggs into the sauce, then return the pan to the fryer and Bake for 2 minutes. Remove the pan from the fryer and stir the eggs into the sauce, whisking them through the sauce. Don't mix in completely. Cook for 4-8 minutes more or until the eggs are set. Let cool, then serve.

Cheesy Egg Bites

Servings: 6 | Cooking Time: 35 Minutes

Ingredients:

- ½ cup shredded Muenster cheese
- 5 eggs, beaten
- 3 tbsp sour cream
- ½ tsp dried oregano
- Salt and pepper to taste
- 1/3 cup minced bell pepper
- 3 tbsp minced scallions

Directions:

1. Preheat the air fryer to 325°F. Make a foil sling: Fold an 18-inch-long piece of heavy-duty aluminum foil lengthwise into thirds. Combine the eggs, sour cream, oregano, salt, and pepper in a bowl. Add the bell peppers, scallions, and cheese and stir. Add the mixture to 6 egg bite cups, making sure to get some of the solids in each cup.
2. Put the egg bite pan on the sling you made and lower it into the fryer. Leave the foil in but bend down the edges so they fit. Bake the bites for 10-15 minutes or until a toothpick inserted into the center comes out clean. Remove the egg bite pan using the foil sling. Cool for 5 minutes, then turn the pan upside down over a plate to remove the egg bites. Serve warm.

Orange-glazed Cinnamon Rolls

Cooking Time: 30 Minutes

Ingredients:

- ½ cup + 1 tbsp evaporated cane sugar
- 1 cup Greek yogurt
- 2 cups flour
- 2 tsp baking powder
- ½ tsp salt
- 4 tbsp butter, softened
- 2 tsp ground cinnamon
- 4 oz cream cheese
- ¼ cup orange juice
- 1 tbsp orange zest
- 1 tbsp lemon juice

Directions:

1. Preheat air fryer to 350°F. Grease a baking dish. Combine yogurt, 1 ¾ cups flour, baking powder, salt, and ¼ cup sugar in a large bowl until dough forms. Dust the rest of the flour onto a flat work surface. Transfer the dough on the flour and roll into a ¼-inch thick rectangle. If the dough continues to stick to the rolling pin, add 1 tablespoon of flour and continue to roll.
2. Mix the butter, cinnamon, orange zest and 1 tbsp of sugar in a bowl. Spread the butter mixture evenly over the dough. Roll the dough into a log, starting with the long side. Tuck in the end. Cut the log into 6 equal pieces. Place in the baking dish swirl-side up. The rolls can touch each other. Bake in the air fryer for 10-12 minutes until the rolls are cooked through, and the tops are golden. Let cool for 10 minutes. While the rolls are cooling, combine cream cheese, the rest of the sugar, lemon juice, and orange juice in a small bowl. When the rolls are cool enough, top with glaze and serve.

Apple & Turkey Breakfast Sausages

Servings: 4 | Cooking Time: 15 Minutes

Ingredients:

- ½ tsp coriander seeds, crushed
- 1 tbsp chopped rosemary
- 1 tbsp chopped thyme
- Salt and pepper to taste
- 1 tsp fennel seeds, crushed
- ¾ tsp smoked paprika
- ½ tsp garlic powder
- ½ tsp shallot powder
- ⅛ tsp red pepper flakes
- 1 pound ground turkey
- ½ cup minced apples

Directions:

1. Combine all of the seasonings in a bowl. Add turkey and apple and blend seasonings in well with your hands. Form patties about 3 inches in diameter and ¼ inch thick.
2. Preheat air fryer to 400°F. Arrange patties in a single layer on the greased frying basket. Air Fry for 10 minutes, flipping once until brown and cooked through. Serve.

Aromatic Mushroom Omelet

Servings: 4 | Cooking Time: 30 Minutes

Ingredients:

- 6 eggs
- 2 tbsp milk
- ½ yellow onion, diced
- ½ cup diced mushrooms
- 2 tbsp chopped parsley
- 1 tsp dried oregano
- 1 tbsp chopped chives
- ½ tbsp chopped dill
- ½ cup grated Gruyère cheese

Directions:

1. Preheat air fryer to 350°F. Beat eggs in a medium bowl, then add the rest of the ingredients, except for the parsley. Stir until completely combined. Pour the mixture into a greased pan and bake in the air fryer for 18-20 minutes until the eggs are set. Top with parsley and serve.

Appetizers And Snacks Recipes

Asian-style Shrimp Toast

Servings: 4 | Cooking Time: 25 Minutes

Ingredients:

- 8 large raw shrimp, chopped
- 1 egg white
- 2 garlic cloves, minced
- 1 red chili, minced
- 1 celery stalk, minced
- 2 tbsp cornstarch
- ¼ tsp Chinese five-spice
- 3 firm bread slices

Directions:

1. Preheat air fryer to 350°F. Add the shrimp, egg white, garlic, red chili, celery, corn starch, and five-spice powder in a bowl and combine. Place 1/3 of the shrimp mix on a slice of bread, smearing it to the edges, then slice the bread into 4 strips. Lay the strips in the frying basket in a single layer and Air Fry for 3-6 minutes until golden and crispy. Repeat until all strips are cooked. Serve hot.

Garlic Wings

Servings: 4 | Cooking Time: 15 Minutes

Ingredients:

- 2 pounds chicken wings
- oil for misting
- cooking spray
- Marinade
- 1 cup buttermilk
- 2 cloves garlic, mashed flat
- 1 teaspoon Worcestershire sauce
- 1 bay leaf
- Coating
- 1½ cups grated Parmesan cheese
- ¾ cup breadcrumbs
- 1½ tablespoons garlic powder
- ½ teaspoon salt

Directions:

1. Mix all marinade ingredients together.
2. Remove wing tips (the third joint) and discard or freeze for stock. Cut the remaining wings at the joint and toss them into the marinade, stirring to coat well. Refrigerate for at least an hour but no more than 8 hours.
3. When ready to cook, combine all coating ingredients in a shallow dish.
4. Remove wings from marinade, shaking off excess, and roll in coating mixture. Press coating into wings so that it sticks well. Spray wings with oil.
5. Spray air fryer basket with cooking spray. Place wings in basket in single layer, close but not touching.
6. Cook at 360°F for 15minutes or until chicken is done and juices run clear.
7. Repeat previous step to cook remaining wings.

Jalapeño Poppers

Servings: 18 | Cooking Time: 5 Minutes

Ingredients:

- ½ pound jalapeño peppers
- ¼ cup cornstarch
- 1 egg
- 1 tablespoon lime juice
- ¼ cup plain breadcrumbs
- ¼ cup panko breadcrumbs
- ½ teaspoon salt
- oil for misting or cooking spray
- Filling
- 4 ounces cream cheese
- 1 teaspoon grated lime zest
- ¼ teaspoon chile powder
- ⅛ teaspoon garlic powder
- ¼ teaspoon salt

Directions:

1. Combine all filling ingredients in small bowl and mix well. Refrigerate while preparing peppers.
2. Cut jalapeños into ½-inch lengthwise slices. Use a small, sharp knife to remove seeds and veins.
3. a. For mild appetizers, discard seeds and veins.
4. b. For hot appetizers, finely chop seeds and veins. Stir a small amount into filling, taste, and continue adding a little at a time until filling is as hot as you like.
5. Stuff each pepper slice with filling.
6. Place cornstarch in a shallow dish.
7. In another shallow dish, beat together egg and lime juice.
8. Place breadcrumbs and salt in a third shallow dish and stir together.
9. Dip each pepper slice in cornstarch, shake off ex-

cess, then dip in egg mixture.
10. Roll in breadcrumbs, pressing to make coating stick.
11. Place pepper slices on a plate in single layer and freeze them for 30minutes.
12. Preheat air fryer to 390°F.
13. Spray frozen peppers with oil or cooking spray. Place in air fryer basket in a single layer and cook for 5minutes.

Kale Chips

Servings: 2 | Cooking Time: 5 Minutes

Ingredients:

- 4 Medium kale leaves, about 1 ounce each
- 2 teaspoons Olive oil
- 2 teaspoons Regular or low-sodium soy sauce or gluten-free tamari sauce

Directions:

1. Preheat the air fryer to 400°F.
2. Cut the stems from the leaves (all the stems, all the way up the leaf). Tear each leaf into three pieces. Put them in a large bowl.
3. Add the olive oil and soy or tamari sauce. Toss well to coat. You can even gently rub the leaves along the side of the bowl to get the liquids to stick to them.
4. When the machine is at temperature, put the leaf pieces in the basket in one layer. Air-fry for 5 minutes, turning and rearranging with kitchen tongs once halfway through, until the chips are dried out and crunchy. Watch carefully so they don't turn dark brown at the edges.
5. Gently pour the contents of the basket onto a wire rack. Cool for at least 5 minutes before serving. The chips can keep for up to 8 hours uncovered on the rack (provided it's not a humid day).

Spicy Chicken And Pepper Jack Cheese Bites

Servings: 8 | Cooking Time: 8 Minutes

Ingredients:

- 8 ounces cream cheese, softened
- 2 cups grated pepper jack cheese
- 1 Jalapeño pepper, diced
- 2 scallions, minced
- 1 teaspoon paprika
- 2 teaspoons salt, divided
- 3 cups shredded cooked chicken
- ¼ cup all-purpose flour*
- 2 eggs, lightly beaten
- 1 cup panko breadcrumbs*
- olive oil, in a spray bottle
- salsa

Directions:

1. Beat the cream cheese in a bowl until it is smooth and easy to stir. Add the pepper jack cheese, Jalapeño pepper, scallions, paprika and 1 teaspoon of salt. Fold in the shredded cooked chicken and combine well. Roll this mixture into 1-inch balls.
2. Set up a dredging station with three shallow dishes. Place the flour into one shallow dish. Place the eggs into a second shallow dish. Finally, combine the panko breadcrumbs and remaining teaspoon of salt in a third dish.
3. Coat the chicken cheese balls by rolling each ball in the flour first, then dip them into the eggs and finally roll them in the panko breadcrumbs to coat all sides. Refrigerate for at least 30 minutes.
4. Preheat the air fryer to 400°F.
5. Spray the chicken cheese balls with oil and air-fry in batches for 8 minutes. Shake the basket a few times throughout the cooking process to help the balls brown evenly.
6. Serve hot with salsa on the side.

Parmesan Eggplant Bites

Servings:4 | Cooking Time: 35 Minutes

Ingredients:

- 2 eggs
- 2 tbsp heavy cream
- ½ cup bread crumbs
- ½ tsp Italian seasoning
- ½ cup grated Parmesan
- ½ tsp salt
- 1 eggplant, cut into sticks
- ½ cup tomato sauce, warm

Directions:

1. Preheat air fryer to 400ºF. In a bowl, mix the eggs and heavy cream. In another bowl, combine bread crumbs, Parmesan cheese, Italian seasoning and salt. Dip eggplant fries in egg mixture and dredge them in crumb mixture.
2. Place the fries in the greased frying basket and Air Fry for 12 minutes, shaking once. Transfer to a large serving plate and serve with warmed tomato sauce.

Rich Egg-fried Cauliflower Rice

Servings: 4 | Cooking Time: 45 Minutes

Ingredients:

- 2 ½ cups riced cauliflower
- 2 tsp sesame oil
- 1 green bell pepper, diced
- 1 cup peas
- 1 cup diced carrots
- 2 spring onions
- Salt and pepper to taste
- 1 tbsp tamari sauce
- 2 eggs, scrambled

Directions:

1. Preheat air fryer to 370°F. Combine riced cauliflower, bell pepper, peas, carrots, and spring onions in a large bowl. Stir in 1 tsp of sesame oil, salt, and pepper. Grease a baking pan with the remaining tsp of sesame oil. Transfer the rice mixture to the pan and place in the air fryer. Bake for 10 minutes. Remove the pan and drizzle with tamari sauce. Stir in scrambled eggs and serve warm.

Crunchy Spicy Chickpeas

Servings: 6 | Cooking Time: 12 Minutes

Ingredients:

- 2½ cups Canned chickpeas, drained and rinsed
- 2½ tablespoons Vegetable or canola oil
- up to 1 tablespoon Cajun or jerk dried seasoning blend (see here for a Cajun blend, here for a jerk blend)
- up to ¾ teaspoon Table salt (optional)

Directions:

1. Preheat the air fryer to 400°F.
2. Toss the chickpeas, oil, seasoning blend, and salt (if using) in a large bowl until the chickpeas are evenly coated.
3. When the machine is at temperature, pour the chickpeas into the basket. Air-fry for 12 minutes, removing the basket at the 4- and 8-minute marks to toss and rearrange the chickpeas, until very aromatic and perhaps sizzling but not burned.
4. Pour the chickpeas into a large serving bowl. Cool for a couple of minutes, gently stirring once, before you dive in.

Spinach Cups

Servings: 30 | Cooking Time: 5 Minutes

Ingredients:

- 1 6-ounce can crabmeat, drained to yield ⅓ cup meat
- ¼ cup frozen spinach, thawed, drained, and chopped
- 1 clove garlic, minced
- ½ cup grated Parmesan cheese
- 3 tablespoons plain yogurt
- ¼ teaspoon lemon juice
- ½ teaspoon Worcestershire sauce
- 30 mini phyllo shells (2 boxes of 15 each), thawed
- cooking spray

Directions:

1. Remove any bits of shell that might remain in the crabmeat.
2. Mix crabmeat, spinach, garlic, and cheese together.
3. Stir in the yogurt, lemon juice, and Worcestershire sauce and mix well.
4. Spoon a teaspoon of filling into each phyllo shell.
5. Spray air fryer basket and arrange half the shells in the basket.
6. Cook at 390°F for 5minutes.
7. Repeat with remaining shells.

Cheeseburger Slider Pockets

Servings: 4 | Cooking Time: 13 Minutes

Ingredients:

- 1 pound extra lean ground beef
- 2 teaspoons steak seasoning
- 2 tablespoons Worcestershire sauce
- 8 ounces Cheddar cheese
- ⅓ cup ketchup
- ¼ cup light mayonnaise
- 1 tablespoon pickle relish
- 1 pound frozen bread dough, defrosted
- 1 egg, beaten
- sesame seeds
- vegetable or olive oil, in a spray bottle

Directions:

1. Combine the ground beef, steak seasoning and Worcestershire sauce in a large bowl. Divide the meat mixture into 12 equal portions. Cut the Cheddar cheese into twelve 2-inch squares, about ¼-inch thick. Stuff a square of cheese into the center of each portion of meat and shape into a 3-inch patty.
2. Make the slider sauce by combining the ketchup, mayonnaise, and relish in a small bowl. Set aside.

3. Cut the bread dough into twelve pieces. Shape each piece of dough into a ball and use a rolling pin to roll them out into 4-inch circles. Dollop ½ teaspoon of the slider sauce into the center of each dough circle. Place a beef patty on top of the sauce and wrap the dough around the patty, pinching the dough together to seal the pocket shut. Try not to stretch the dough too much when bringing the edges together. Brush both sides of the slider pocket with the beaten egg. Sprinkle sesame seeds on top of each pocket.
4. Preheat the air fryer to 350°F.
5. Spray or brush the bottom of the air fryer basket with oil. Air-fry the slider pockets four at a time. Transfer the slider pockets to the air fryer basket, seam side down and air-fry at 350°F for 10 minutes, until the dough is golden brown. Flip the slider pockets over and air-fry for another 3 minutes. When all the batches are done, pop all the sliders into the air fryer for a few minutes to re-heat and serve them hot out of the fryer.

Cheddar-pimiento Strips

Servings: 4 | Cooking Time: 35 Minutes

Ingredients:

- 8 oz shredded sharp cheddar cheese
- 1 jar chopped pimientos, including juice
- ¼ cup mayonnaise
- ¼ cup cream cheese
- Salt and pepper to taste
- 1 tsp chopped parsley
- 8 slices sandwich bread
- 4 tbsp butter, melted

Directions:

1. In a bowl, mix the cheddar cheese, cream cheese, pimientos, mayonnaise, salt, parsley and pepper. Let chill covered in the fridge for 30 minutes.
2. Preheat air fryer at 350ºF. Spread pimiento mixture over 4 bread slices, then top with the remaining slices and press down just enough to not smoosh cheese out of sandwiches edges. Brush the top and bottom of each sandwich lightly with melted butter. Place sandwiches in the frying basket and Grill for 6 minutes, flipping once. Slice each sandwich into 16 sections and serve warm.

Spanish Fried Baby Squid

Servings: 2 | Cooking Time: 30 Minutes

Ingredients:

- 1 cup baby squid
- ½ cup semolina flour
- ½ tsp Spanish paprika
- ½ tsp garlic powder
- 2 eggs
- Salt and pepper to taste
- 2 tbsp lemon juice
- 1 tsp Old Bay seasoning

Directions:

1. Preheat air fryer to 350°F. Beat the eggs in a bowl. Stir in lemon juice and set aside. Mix flour, Old Bay seasoning, garlic powder, paprika, salt, and pepper in another bowl. Dip each piece of squid into the flour, then into the eggs, and then again. Transfer them to the greased frying basket and Air Fry for 18-20 minutes, shaking the basket occasionally until crispy and golden brown. Serve hot.

Garlic-herb Pita Chips

Servings: 4 | Cooking Time: 6 Minutes

Ingredients:

- ¼ teaspoon dried basil
- ¼ teaspoon marjoram
- ¼ teaspoon ground oregano
- ¼ teaspoon garlic powder
- ¼ teaspoon ground thyme
- ¼ teaspoon salt
- 2 whole 6-inch pitas, whole grain or white
- oil for misting or cooking spray

Directions:

1. Mix all seasonings together.
2. Cut each pita half into 4 wedges. Break apart wedges at the fold.
3. Mist one side of pita wedges with oil. Sprinkle with half of seasoning mix.
4. Turn pita wedges over, mist the other side with oil, and sprinkle with remaining seasonings.
5. Place pita wedges in air fryer basket and cook at 330°F for 2minutes.
6. Shake basket and cook for 2minutes longer. Shake again, and if needed cook for 2 moreminutes, until crisp. Watch carefully because at this point they will cook very quickly.

Parmesan Pizza Nuggets

Servings: 8 | Cooking Time: 6 Minutes

Ingredients:

- ¾ cup warm filtered water
- 1 package fast-rising yeast
- ½ teaspoon salt
- 2 cups all-purpose flour
- ¼ cup finely grated Parmesan cheese
- 1 teaspoon Italian seasoning
- 2 tablespoon extra-virgin olive oil
- 1 teaspoon kosher salt

Directions:

1. Preheat the air fryer to 370°F.
2. In a large microwave-safe bowl, add the water. Heat for 40 seconds in the microwave. Remove and mix in the yeast and salt. Let sit 5 minutes.
3. Meanwhile, in a medium bowl, mix the flour with the Parmesan cheese and Italian seasoning. Set aside.
4. Using a stand mixer with a dough hook attachment, add the yeast liquid and then mix in the flour mixture ⅓ cup at a time until all the flour mixture is added and a dough is formed.
5. Remove the bowl from the stand, and then let the dough rise for 1 hour in a warm space, covered with a kitchen towel.
6. After the dough has doubled in size, remove it from the bowl and punch it down a few times on a lightly floured flat surface.
7. Divide the dough into 4 balls, and then roll each ball out into a long, skinny, sticklike shape.
8. Using a sharp knife, cut each dough stick into 6 pieces. Repeat for the remaining dough balls until you have about 24 nuggets formed.
9. Lightly brush the top of each bite with the egg whites and cover with a pinch of sea salt.
10. Spray the air fryer basket with olive oil spray and place the pizza nuggets on top. Cook for 6 minutes, or until lightly browned. Remove and keep warm.
11. Repeat until all the nuggets are cooked.
12. Serve warm.

Fried Gyoza

Servings: 18 | Cooking Time: 6 Minutes

Ingredients:

- 5 ounces Lean ground pork
- 2½ tablespoons Very thinly sliced scallion
- 1 tablespoon plus 2 teaspoons Minced peeled fresh ginger
- 1¼ teaspoons Toasted sesame oil
- ⅛ teaspoon Table salt
- ⅛ teaspoon Ground black pepper
- 18 Round gyoza or square wonton wrappers (thawed, if necessary)
- Vegetable oil spray

Directions:

1. Preheat the air fryer to 350°F .
2. Mix the ground pork, scallion, ginger, sesame oil, salt, and pepper in a bowl until well combined.
3. Set a bowl of water on a clean, dry surface or next to a clean, dry cutting board. Set one gyoza or wonton wrapper on that surface. Dip your clean finger in the water and run it around the perimeter of the gyoza wrapper or the edge of the wonton wrapper. Put about 1 ½ teaspoons of the meat mixture in the center of the wrapper.
4. For the gyoza wrapper, fold the wrapper in half to close, pressing the edge to seal, then wet the outside of the edge of both sides of the seam and pleat it into little ridges to seal.
5. For the wonton wrapper, fold it in half lengthwise to make a rectangle, then seal the sides together, flattening the packet a bit as you do.
6. Set the filled wrapper aside and continue making more in the same way. When done, generously coat them on all sides with vegetable oil spray.
7. Place the gyoza in the basket in one layer and air-fry undisturbed for 6 minutes, or until browned and crisp at the edges.
8. Use kitchen tongs or a nonstick-safe spatula to gently transfer the gyoza to a wire rack. Cool for only 2 or 3 minutes before serving hot.

Tasty Roasted Black Olives & Tomatoes

Servings: 6 | Cooking Time: 25 Minutes

Ingredients:

- 2 cups grape tomatoes
- 4 garlic cloves, chopped
- ½ red onion, chopped
- 1 cup black olives
- 1 cup green olives
- 1 tbsp thyme, minced
- 1 tbsp oregano, minced
- 2 tbsp olive oil
- ½ tsp salt

Directions:

1. Preheat air fryer to 380°F. Add all ingredients to a bowl and toss well to coat. Pour the mixture into the frying basket and Roast for 10 minutes. Stir the mixture, then Roast for an additional 10 minutes. Serve and enjoy!

"fried" Pickles With Homemade Ranch

Servings: 8 | Cooking Time: 8 Minutes

Ingredients:

- 1 cup all-purpose flour
- 2 teaspoons dried dill
- ½ teaspoon paprika
- ¾ cup buttermilk
- 1 egg
- 4 large kosher dill pickles, sliced ¼-inch thick
- 2 cups panko breadcrumbs

Directions:

1. Preheat the air fryer to 380°F.
2. In a medium bowl, whisk together the flour, dill, paprika, buttermilk, and egg.
3. Dip and coat thick slices of dill pickles into the batter. Next, dredge into the panko breadcrumbs.
4. Place a single layer of breaded pickles into the air fryer basket. Spray the pickles with cooking spray. Cook for 4 minutes, turn over, and cook another 4 minutes. Repeat until all the pickle chips have been cooked.

Tomato & Halloumi Bruschetta

Servings: 4 | Cooking Time: 20 Minutes

Ingredients:

- 2 tbsp softened butter
- 8 French bread slices
- 1 cup grated halloumi cheese
- ½ cup basil pesto
- 12 chopped cherry tomatoes
- 2 green onions, thinly sliced

Directions:

1. Preheat air fryer to 350°F. Spread butter on one side of the bread. Place butter-side up in the frying basket. Bake until the bread is slightly brown, 3-5 minutes. Remove the bread and top it with halloumi cheese. Melt the cheese on the bread in the air fryer for another 1-3 minutes.
2. Meanwhile, mix pesto, cherry tomatoes, and green onions in a small bowl. When the cheese has melted, take the bread out of the fryer and arrange on a plate. Top with pesto mix and serve.

Cheese Arancini

Servings: 8 | Cooking Time: 12 Minutes

Ingredients:

- 1 cup Water
- ½ cup Raw white Arborio rice
- 1½ teaspoons Butter
- ¼ teaspoon Table salt
- 8 ¾-inch semi-firm mozzarella cubes (not fresh mozzarella)
- 2 Large egg(s), well beaten
- 1 cup Seasoned Italian-style dried bread crumbs (gluten-free, if a concern)
- Olive oil spray

Directions:

1. Combine the water, rice, butter, and salt in a small saucepan. Bring to a boil over medium-high heat, stirring occasionally. Cover, reduce the heat to very low, and simmer very slowly for 20 minutes.
2. Take the saucepan off the heat and let it stand, covered, for 10 minutes. Uncover it and fluff the rice. Cool for 20 minutes. (The rice can be made up to 1 hour in advance; keep it covered in its saucepan.)
3. Preheat the air fryer to 375°F .
4. Set up and fill two shallow soup plates or small bowls on your counter: one with the beaten egg(s) and one with the bread crumbs.

5. With clean but wet hands, scoop up about 2 tablespoons of the cooked rice and form it into a ball. Push a cube of mozzarella into the middle of the ball and seal the cheese inside. Dip the ball in the egg(s) to coat completely, letting any excess egg slip back into the rest. Roll the ball in the bread crumbs to coat evenly but lightly. Set aside and continue making more rice balls.
6. Generously spray the balls with olive oil spray, then set them in the basket in one layer. They must not touch. Air-fry undisturbed for 10 minutes, or until crunchy and golden brown. If the machine is at 360°F, you may need to add 2 minutes to the cooking time.
7. Use a nonstick-safe spatula, and maybe a flatware spoon for balance, to gently transfer the balls to a wire rack. Cool for at least 5 minutes or up to 20 minutes before serving.

Middle Eastern Roasted Chickpeas

Servings: 3 | Cooking Time: 30 Minutes

Ingredients:

- 2 tsp olive oil
- 1 can chickpeas
- Salt to taste
- 1 tsp za'atar seasoning
- 1 tsp ground sumac
- ¼ tsp garlic powder
- 1 tbsp cilantro, chopped

Directions:

1. Combine salt, za'atar, sumac, and garlic powder in a bowl. Preheat air fryer to 375°F. Put half of the chickpeas in the greased frying basket. Bake for 12 minutes, shaking every 5 minutes until crunchy and golden brown. Transfer the chickpeas to a bowl. Lightly coat them with olive oil, then toss them with half of the spice mix while they are still hot. Serve topped with cilantro.

Turkey Bacon Dates

Servings: 16 | Cooking Time: 7 Minutes

Ingredients:

- 16 whole, pitted dates
- 16 whole almonds
- 6 to 8 strips turkey bacon

Directions:

1. Stuff each date with a whole almond.
2. Depending on the size of your stuffed dates, cut bacon strips into halves or thirds. Each strip should be long enough to wrap completely around a date.
3. Wrap each date in a strip of bacon with ends overlapping and secure with toothpicks.
4. Place in air fryer basket and cook at 390°F for 7 minutes, until bacon is as crispy as you like.
5. Drain on paper towels or wire rack. Serve hot or at room temperature.

Garlic Parmesan Kale Chips

Servings: 2 | Cooking Time: 6 Minutes

Ingredients:

- 16 large kale leaves, washed and thick stems removed
- 1 tablespoon avocado oil
- ½ teaspoon garlic powder
- 1 teaspoon soy sauce or tamari
- ¼ cup grated Parmesan cheese

Directions:

1. Preheat the air fryer to 370°F.
2. Make a stack of kale leaves and cut them into 4 pieces.
3. Place the kale pieces into a large bowl. Drizzle the avocado oil onto the kale and rub to coat. Add the garlic powder, soy sauce or tamari, and cheese, tossing to coat.
4. Pour the chips into the air fryer basket and cook for 3 minutes, shake the basket, and cook another 3 minutes, checking for crispness every minute. When done cooking, pour the kale chips onto paper towels and cool at least 5 minutes before serving.

Stuffed Prunes In Bacon

Servings: 6 | Cooking Time: 20 Minutes

Ingredients:

- 12 bacon slices, halved
- 24 pitted prunes
- 3 tbsp crumbled blue cheese
- 1 tbsp cream cheese

Directions:

1. Cut prunes in half lengthwise, but do not cut all the way through. Add ½ tsp of blue cheese and cream cheese to the center of each prune. Wrap each prune with a slice of bacon and seal with a toothpick.
2. Preheat air fryer to 400°F. Place the prunes on the bottom of the greased frying basket in a single layer. Bake for 6-8 minutes, flipping the prunes once until the bacon is cooked and crispy. Allow to cool and serve warm.

Crunchy Parmesan Edamame

Servings:4 | Cooking Time: 25 Minutes + Cooling Time

Ingredients:

- 1 cup edamame, shelled
- 1 tbsp sesame oil
- 1 tsp five-spice powder
- ½ tsp salt
- ½ tsp garlic powder
- ¼ cup grated Parmesan

Directions:

1. Cook the edamame in boiling salted water until crisp-tender, about 10 minutes. Drain and leave to cool. Preheat air fryer to 350ºF. Combine edamame, garlic, and sesame oil in a bowl. Place them in the frying basket and Air Fry for 16 minutes, shaking twice. Transfer to a small bowl and toss with five-spice powder and salt. Serve chilled topped with Parmesan cheese. Enjoy!

Grilled Ham & Muenster Cheese On Raisin Bread

Servings: 1 | Cooking Time: 10 Minutes

Ingredients:

- 2 slices raisin bread
- 2 tablespoons butter, softened
- 2 teaspoons honey mustard
- 3 slices thinly sliced honey ham (about 3 ounces)
- 4 slices Muenster cheese (about 3 ounces)
- 2 toothpicks

Directions:

1. Preheat the air fryer to 370°F.
2. Spread the softened butter on one side of both slices of raisin bread and place the bread, buttered side down on the counter. Spread the honey mustard on the other side of each slice of bread. Layer 2 slices of cheese, the ham and the remaining 2 slices of cheese on one slice of bread and top with the other slice of bread. Remember to leave the buttered side of the bread on the outside.
3. Transfer the sandwich to the air fryer basket and secure the sandwich with toothpicks.
4. Air-fry at 370°F for 5 minutes. Flip the sandwich over, remove the toothpicks and air-fry for another 5 minutes. Cut the sandwich in half and enjoy!!

Curried Veggie Samosas

Servings: 4 | Cooking Time: 30 Minutes

Ingredients:

- 4 cooked potatoes, mashed
- ¼ cup peas
- 2 tsp coconut oil
- 3 garlic cloves, minced
- 1 ½ tbsp lemon juice
- 1 ½ tsp cumin powder
- 1 tsp onion powder
- 1 tsp ground coriander
- Salt to taste
- ½ tsp curry powder
- ¼ tsp cayenne powder
- 10 rice paper wrappers
- 1 cup cilantro chutney

Directions:

1. Preheat air fryer to 390°F. In a bowl, place the mashed potatoes, peas, oil, garlic, lemon juice, cumin, onion powder, coriander, salt, curry powder, and cayenne. Stir.

2. Fill a bowl with water. Soak a rice paper wrapper in the water for a few seconds. Lay it on a flat surface. Place ¼ cup of the potato filling in the center of the wrapper and roll like a burrito or spring roll. Repeat the process until you run out of ingredients. Place the "samosas" inside in the greased frying basket, separating them. Air Fry for 8-10 minutes or until hot and crispy around the edges. Let cool for a few minutes. Enjoy with the cilantro chutney.

Tempura Fried Veggies

Servings: 4 | Cooking Time: 6 Minutes

Ingredients:

- ½ cup all-purpose flour
- ½ teaspoon black pepper
- ¼ teaspoon salt
- 2 large eggs
- 1¼ cups panko breadcrumbs
- 1 tablespoon extra-virgin olive oil
- 1 cup white button mushrooms, cleaned
- 1 medium zucchini, skinned and sliced
- 1 medium carrot, skinned sliced

Directions:

1. Preheat the air fryer to 400°F.
2. In a small bowl, mix the flour, pepper, and salt.
3. In a separate bowl, whisk the eggs.
4. In a third bowl, mix together the breadcrumbs and olive oil.
5. Begin to batter the vegetables by placing them one at a time into the flour, then dipping them in the eggs, and coating them in breadcrumbs. When you've prepared enough to begin air frying, liberally spray the air fryer basket with olive oil and place the vegetables inside.
6. Cook for 6 minutes, or until the breadcrumb coating on the outside appears golden brown. Repeat coating the other vegetables while the first batch is cooking.
7. When the cooking completes, carefully remove the vegetables and keep them warm. Repeat cooking for the remaining vegetables until all are cooked.
8. Serve warm.

Cauliflower "tater" Tots

Servings: 6 | Cooking Time: 10 Minutes

Ingredients:

- 1 head of cauliflower
- 2 eggs
- ¼ cup all-purpose flour*
- ½ cup grated Parmesan cheese
- 1 teaspoon salt
- freshly ground black pepper
- vegetable or olive oil, in a spray bottle

Directions:

1. Grate the head of cauliflower with a box grater or finely chop it in a food processor. You should have about 3½ cups. Place the chopped cauliflower in the center of a clean kitchen towel and twist the towel tightly to squeeze all the water out of the cauliflower. (This can be done in two batches to make it easier to drain all the water from the cauliflower.)
2. Place the squeezed cauliflower in a large bowl. Add the eggs, flour, Parmesan cheese, salt and freshly ground black pepper. Shape the cauliflower into small cylinders or "tater tot" shapes, rolling roughly one tablespoon of the mixture at a time. Place the tots on a cookie sheet lined with paper towel to absorb any residual moisture. Spray the cauliflower tots all over with oil.
3. Preheat the air fryer to 400°F.
4. Air-fry the tots at 400°F, one layer at a time for 10 minutes, turning them over for the last few minutes of the cooking process for even browning. Season with salt and black pepper. Serve hot with your favorite dipping sauce.

Baba Ghanouj

Servings: 2 | Cooking Time: 40 Minutes

Ingredients:

- 2 Small (12-ounce) purple Italian eggplant(s)
- ¼ cup Olive oil
- ¼ cup Tahini
- ½ teaspoon Ground black pepper
- ¼ teaspoon Onion powder
- ¼ teaspoon Mild smoked paprika (optional)
- Up to 1 teaspoon Table salt

Directions:

1. Preheat the air fryer to 400°F.
2. Prick the eggplant(s) on all sides with a fork. When the machine is at temperature, set the eggplant(s) in the basket in one layer. Air-fry undisturbed for 40 minutes, or until blackened and soft.
3. Remove the basket from the machine. Cool the eggplant(s) in the basket for 20 minutes.
4. Use a nonstick-safe spatula, and perhaps a flatware tablespoon for balance, to gently transfer the eggplant(s) to a bowl. The juices will run out. Make sure the bowl is close to the basket. Split the eggplant(s) open.
5. Scrape the soft insides of half an eggplant into a food processor. Repeat with the remaining piece(s). Add any juices from the bowl to the eggplant in the food processor, but discard the skins and stems.
6. Add the olive oil, tahini, pepper, onion powder, and smoked paprika (if using). Add about half the salt, then cover and process until smooth, stopping the machine at least once to scrape down the inside of the canister. Check the spread for salt and add more as needed. Scrape the baba ghanouj into a bowl and serve warm, or set aside at room temperature for up to 2 hours, or cover and store in the refrigerator for up to 4 days.

Dijon Chicken Wings

Servings: 6 | Cooking Time: 60 Minutes

Ingredients:

- 2 lb chicken wings, split at the joint
- 1 tbsp water
- 1 tbs salt
- 1 tsp black pepper
- 1 tsp red chili powder
- 1 tbsp butter, melted
- 1 tbsp Dijon mustard
- 2 tbsp yellow mustard
- ¼ cup honey
- 1 tsp apple cider vinegar
- Salt to taste

Directions:

1. Preheat air fryer at 250ºF. Pour water in the bottom of the frying basket to ensure minimum smoke from fat drippings. Sprinkle the chicken wings with salt, pepper, and red chili powder. Place chicken wings in the greased frying basket and Air Fry for 12 minutes, tossing once. Whisk the remaining ingredients in a bowl. Add in chicken wings and toss to coat. Serve immediately.

Desserts And Sweets Recipes

Party S′mores

Servings: 6 | Cooking Time: 15 Minutes

Ingredients:

- 2 dark chocolate bars, cut into 12 pieces
- 12 buttermilk biscuits
- 12 marshmallows

Directions:

1. Preheat air fryer to 350°F. Place 6 biscuits in the air fryer. Top each square with a piece of dark chocolate. Bake for 2 minutes. Add a marshmallow to each piece of chocolate. Cook for another minute. Remove and top with another piece of biscuit. Serve warm.

Thumbprint Sugar Cookies

Servings: 10 | Cooking Time: 8 Minutes

Ingredients:

- 2½ tablespoons butter
- ⅓ cup cane sugar
- 1 teaspoon pure vanilla extract
- 1 large egg
- 1 cup all-purpose flour
- ½ teaspoon baking soda
- ¼ teaspoon salt
- 10 chocolate kisses

Directions:

1. Preheat the air fryer to 350°F.
2. In a large bowl, cream the butter with the sugar and vanilla. Whisk in the egg and set aside.
3. In a separate bowl, mix the flour, baking soda, and salt. Then gently mix the dry ingredients into the wet. Portion the dough into 10 balls; then press down on each with the bottom of a cup to create a flat cookie.
4. Liberally spray the metal trivet of an air fryer basket with olive oil mist.
5. Place the cookies in the air fryer basket on the trivet and cook for 8 minutes or until the tops begin to lightly brown.
6. Remove and immediately press the chocolate kisses into the tops of the cookies while still warm.
7. Let cool 5 minutes and then enjoy.

Easy Churros

Servings: 12 | Cooking Time: 10 Minutes

Ingredients:

- ½ cup Water
- 4 tablespoons (¼ cup/½ stick) Butter
- ¼ teaspoon Table salt
- ½ cup All-purpose flour
- 2 Large egg(s)
- ¼ cup Granulated white sugar
- 2 teaspoons Ground cinnamon

Directions:

1. Bring the water, butter, and salt to a boil in a small saucepan set over high heat, stirring occasionally.
2. When the butter has fully melted, reduce the heat to medium and stir in the flour to form a dough. Continue cooking, stirring constantly, to dry out the dough until it coats the bottom and sides of the pan with a film, even a crust. Remove the pan from the heat, scrape the dough into a bowl, and cool for 15 minutes.
3. Using an electric hand mixer at medium speed, beat in the egg, or eggs one at a time, until the dough is smooth and firm enough to hold its shape.
4. Mix the sugar and cinnamon in a small bowl. Scoop up 1 tablespoon of the dough and roll it in the sugar mixture to form a small, coated tube about ½ inch in diameter and 2 inches long. Set it aside and make 5 more tubes for the small batch or 11 more for the large one.
5. Set the tubes on a plate and freeze for 20 minutes. Meanwhile, Preheat the air fryer to 375°F .
6. Set 3 frozen tubes in the basket for a small batch or 6 for a large one with as much air space between them as possible. Air-fry undisturbed for 10 minutes, or until puffed, brown, and set.
7. Use kitchen tongs to transfer the churros to a wire rack to cool for at least 5 minutes. Meanwhile, air-fry and cool the second batch of churros in the same way.

Strawberry Donuts

Servings: 4 | Cooking Time: 55 Minutes

Ingredients:

- ¾ cup Greek yogurt
- 2 tbsp maple syrup
- 1 tbsp vanilla extract
- 2 tsp active dry yeast
- 1 ½ cups all-purpose flour
- 3 tbsp milk
- ½ cup strawberry jam

Directions:

1. Preheat air fryer to 350°F. Whisk the Greek yogurt, maple syrup, vanilla extract, and yeast until well combined. Then toss in flour until you get a sticky dough. Let rest covered for 10 minutes. Flour a parchment paper on a flat surface, lay the dough, sprinkle with some flour, and flatten to ½-inch thick with a rolling pin.
2. Using a 3-inch cookie cutter, cut the donuts. Repeat the process until no dough is left. Place the donuts in the basket and let rise for 15-20 minutes. Spread some milk on top of each donut and Air Fry for 4 minutes. Turn the donuts, spread more milk, and Air Fry for 4 more minutes until golden brown. Let cool for 15 minutes. Using a knife, cut the donuts 3/4 lengthwise, brush 1 tbsp of strawberry jam on each and close them. Serve.

Chocolate Soufflés

Servings: 2 | Cooking Time: 14 Minutes

Ingredients:

- butter and sugar for greasing the ramekins
- 3 ounces semi-sweet chocolate, chopped
- ¼ cup unsalted butter
- 2 eggs, yolks and white separated
- 3 tablespoons sugar
- ½ teaspoon pure vanilla extract
- 2 tablespoons all-purpose flour
- powdered sugar, for dusting the finished soufflés
- heavy cream, for serving

Directions:

1. Butter and sugar two 6-ounce ramekins. (Butter the ramekins and then coat the butter with sugar by shaking it around in the ramekin and dumping out any excess.)
2. Melt the chocolate and butter together, either in the microwave or in a double boiler. In a separate bowl, beat the egg yolks vigorously. Add the sugar and the vanilla extract and beat well again. Drizzle in the chocolate and butter, mixing well. Stir in the flour, combining until there are no lumps.
3. Preheat the air fryer to 330°F.
4. In a separate bowl, whisk the egg whites to soft peak stage (the point at which the whites can almost stand up on the end of your whisk). Fold the whipped egg whites into the chocolate mixture gently and in stages.
5. Transfer the batter carefully to the buttered ramekins, leaving about ½-inch at the top. (You may have a little extra batter, depending on how airy the batter is, so you might be able to squeeze out a third soufflé if you want to.) Place the ramekins into the air fryer basket and air-fry for 14 minutes. The soufflés should have risen nicely and be brown on top. (Don't worry if the top gets a little dark – you'll be covering it with powdered sugar in the next step.)
6. Dust with powdered sugar and serve immediately with heavy cream to pour over the top at the table.

Oatmeal Blackberry Crisp

Servings: 6 | Cooking Time: 20 Minutes

Ingredients:

- 1 cup rolled oats
- ½ cup flour
- ¼ cup olive oil
- ¼ tsp salt
- 1 tsp cinnamon
- 1/3 cup honey
- 4 cups blackberries

Directions:

1. Preheat air fryer to 350°F. Combine rolled oats, flour, olive oil, salt, cinnamon, and honey in a large bowl. Mix well. Spread blackberries on the bottom of a greased cooking pan. Cover them with the oat mixture. Place pan in air fryer and Bake for 15 minutes. Cool for a few minutes. Serve and enjoy.

Giant Buttery Oatmeal Cookie

Servings: 4 | Cooking Time: 16 Minutes

Ingredients:

- 1 cup Rolled oats (not quick-cooking or steel-cut oats)
- ½ cup All-purpose flour
- ½ teaspoon Baking soda
- ½ teaspoon Ground cinnamon
- ½ teaspoon Table salt
- 3½ tablespoons Butter, at room temperature
- ⅓ cup Packed dark brown sugar
- 1½ tablespoons Granulated white sugar
- 3 tablespoons (or 1 medium egg, well beaten) Pasteurized egg substitute, such as Egg Beaters
- ¾ teaspoon Vanilla extract
- ⅓ cup Chopped pecans
- Baking spray

Directions:

1. Preheat the air fryer to 350°F .
2. Stir the oats, flour, baking soda, cinnamon, and salt in a bowl until well combined.
3. Using an electric hand mixer at medium speed , beat the butter, brown sugar, and granulated white sugar until creamy and thick, about 3 minutes, scraping down the inside of the bowl occasionally. Beat in the egg substitute or egg (as applicable) and vanilla until uniform.
4. Scrape down and remove the beaters. Fold in the flour mixture and pecans with a rubber spatula just until all the flour is moistened and the nuts are even throughout the dough.
5. For a small air fryer, coat the inside of a 6-inch round cake pan with baking spray. For a medium air fryer, coat the inside of a 7-inch round cake pan with baking spray. And for a large air fryer, coat the inside of an 8-inch round cake pan with baking spray. Scrape and gently press the dough into the prepared pan, spreading it into an even layer to the perimeter.
6. Set the pan in the basket and air-fry undisturbed for 16 minutes, or until puffed and browned.
7. Transfer the pan to a wire rack and cool for 10 minutes. Loosen the cookie from the perimeter with a spatula, then invert the pan onto a cutting board and let the cookie come free. Remove the pan and reinvert the cookie onto the wire rack. Cool for 5 minutes more before slicing into wedges to serve.

Caramel Apple Crumble

Servings: 6 | Cooking Time: 50 Minutes

Ingredients:

- 4 apples, peeled and thinly sliced
- 2 tablespoons sugar
- 1 tablespoon flour
- 1 teaspoon ground cinnamon
- ¼ teaspoon ground allspice
- healthy pinch ground nutmeg
- 10 caramel squares, cut into small pieces
- Crumble Topping:
- ¾ cup rolled oats
- ¼ cup sugar
- ⅓ cup flour
- ¼ teaspoon ground cinnamon
- 6 tablespoons butter, melted

Directions:

1. Preheat the air fryer to 330°F.
2. Combine the apples, sugar, flour, and spices in a large bowl and toss to coat. Add the caramel pieces and mix well. Pour the apple mixture into a 1-quart round baking dish that will fit in your air fryer basket (6-inch diameter).
3. To make the crumble topping, combine the rolled oats, sugar, flour and cinnamon in a small bowl. Add the melted butter and mix well. Top the apples with the crumble mixture. Cover the entire dish with aluminum foil and transfer the dish to the air fryer basket, lowering the dish into the basket using a sling made of aluminum foil (fold a piece of aluminum foil into a strip about 2-inches wide by 24-inches long). Fold the ends of the aluminum foil over the top of the dish before returning the basket to the air fryer.
4. Air-fry at 330°F for 25 minutes. Remove the aluminum foil and continue to air-fry for another 25 minutes. Serve the crumble warm with whipped cream or vanilla ice cream, if desired.

Mini Carrot Cakes

Servings: 6 | Cooking Time: 25 Minutes

Ingredients:

- 1 cup grated carrots
- ¼ cup raw honey
- ¼ cup olive oil
- ½ tsp vanilla extract
- ½ tsp lemon zest
- 1 egg
- ¼ cup applesauce
- 1 1/3 cups flour
- ¾ tsp baking powder
- ½ tsp baking soda
- ½ tsp ground cinnamon
- ¼ tsp ground nutmeg
- ⅛ tsp ground ginger
- ⅛ tsp salt
- ¼ cup chopped hazelnuts
- 2 tbsp chopped sultanas

Directions:

1. Preheat air fryer to 380°F. Combine the carrots, honey, olive oil, vanilla extract, lemon zest, egg, and applesauce in a bowl. Sift the flour, baking powder, baking soda, cinnamon, nutmeg, ginger, and salt in a separate bowl. Add the wet ingredients to the dry ingredients, mixing until just combined. Fold in the hazelnuts and sultanas. Fill greased muffin cups three-quarters full with the batter, and place them in the frying basket. Bake for 10-12 minutes until a toothpick inserted in the center of a cupcake comes out clean. Serve and enjoy!

Peanut Butter Cup Doughnut Holes

Servings: 24 | Cooking Time: 4 Minutes

Ingredients:

- 1½ cups bread flour
- 1 teaspoon active dry yeast
- 1 tablespoon sugar
- ¼ teaspoon salt
- ½ cup warm milk
- ½ teaspoon vanilla extract
- 2 egg yolks
- 2 tablespoons melted butter
- 24 miniature peanut butter cups, plus a few more for garnish
- vegetable oil, in a spray bottle
- Doughnut Topping
- 1 cup chocolate chips
- 2 tablespoons milk

Directions:

1. Combine the flour, yeast, sugar and salt in a bowl. Add the milk, vanilla, egg yolks and butter. Mix well until the dough starts to come together. Transfer the dough to a floured surface and knead by hand for 2 minutes. Shape the dough into a ball and transfer it to a large oiled bowl. Cover the bowl with a towel and let the dough rise in a warm place for 1 to 1½ hours, until the dough has doubled in size.
2. When the dough has risen, punch it down and roll it into a 24-inch long log. Cut the dough into 24 pieces. Push a peanut butter cup into the center of each piece of dough, pinch the dough shut and roll it into a ball. Place the dough balls on a cookie sheet and let them rise in a warm place for 30 minutes.
3. Preheat the air fryer to 400°F.
4. Spray or brush the dough balls lightly with vegetable oil. Air-fry eight at a time, at 400°F for 4 minutes, turning them over halfway through the cooking process.
5. While the doughnuts are air frying, prepare the topping. Place the chocolate chips and milk in a microwave safe bowl. Microwave on high for 1 minute. Stir and microwave for an additional 30 seconds if necessary to get all the chips to melt. Stir until the chips are melted and smooth.
6. Dip the top half of the doughnut holes into the melted chocolate. Place them on a rack to set up for just a few minutes and watch them disappear.

Fried Banana S'mores

Servings: 4 | Cooking Time: 6 Minutes

Ingredients:

- 4 bananas
- 3 tablespoons mini semi-sweet chocolate chips
- 3 tablespoons mini peanut butter chips
- 3 tablespoons mini marshmallows
- 3 tablespoons graham cracker cereal

Directions:

1. Preheat the air fryer to 400°F.
2. Slice into the un-peeled bananas lengthwise along the inside of the curve, but do not slice through the bottom of the peel. Open the banana slightly to form a pocket.
3. Fill each pocket with chocolate chips, peanut butter chips and marshmallows. Poke the graham cracker

cereal into the filling.

4. Place the bananas in the air fryer basket, resting them on the side of the basket and each other to keep them upright with the filling facing up. Air-fry for 6 minutes, or until the bananas are soft to the touch, the peels have blackened and the chocolate and marshmallows have melted and toasted.

5. Let them cool for a couple of minutes and then simply serve with a spoon to scoop out the filling.

Cheese & Honey Stuffed Figs

Servings: 4 | Cooking Time: 15 Minutes

Ingredients:

- 8 figs, stem off
- 2 oz cottage cheese
- ¼ tsp ground cinnamon
- ¼ tsp orange zest
- ¼ tsp vanilla extract
- 2 tbsp honey
- 1 tbsp olive oil

Directions:

1. Preheat air fryer to 360°F. Cut an "X" in the top of each fig 1/3 way through, leaving intact the base. Mix together the cottage cheese, cinnamon, orange zest, vanilla extract and 1 tbsp of honey in a bowl. Spoon the cheese mixture into the cavity of each fig. Put the figs in a single layer in the frying basket. Drizzle the olive oil over the top of the figs and Roast for 10 minutes. Drizzle with the remaining honey. Serve and enjoy!

Fried Pineapple Chunks

Servings: 3 | Cooking Time: 10 Minutes

Ingredients:

- 3 tablespoons Cornstarch
- 1 Large egg white, beaten until foamy
- 1 cup (4 ounces) Ground vanilla wafer cookies (not low-fat cookies)
- ¼ teaspoon Ground dried ginger
- 18 (about 2¼ cups) Fresh 1-inch chunks peeled and cored pineapple

Directions:

1. Preheat the air fryer to 400°F.

2. Put the cornstarch in a medium or large bowl. Put the beaten egg white in a small bowl. Pour the cookie crumbs and ground dried ginger into a large zip-closed plastic bag, shaking it a bit to combine them.

3. Dump the pineapple chunks into the bowl with the cornstarch. Toss and stir until well coated. Use your cleaned fingers or a large fork like a shovel to pick up a few pineapple chunks, shake off any excess cornstarch, and put them in the bowl with the egg white. Stir gently, then pick them up and let any excess egg white slip back into the rest. Put them in the bag with the crumb mixture. Repeat the cornstarch-then-egg process until all the pineapple chunks are in the bag. Seal the bag and shake gently, turning the bag this way and that, to coat the pieces well.

4. Set the coated pineapple chunks in the basket with as much air space between them as possible. Even a fraction of an inch will work, but they should not touch. Air-fry undisturbed for 10 minutes, or until golden brown and crisp.

5. Gently dump the contents of the basket onto a wire rack. Cool for at least 5 minutes or up to 15 minutes before serving.

Cherry Hand Pies

Servings: 8 | Cooking Time: 8 Minutes

Ingredients:

- 4 cups frozen or canned pitted tart cherries (if using canned, drain and pat dry)
- 2 teaspoons lemon juice
- ½ cup sugar
- ¼ cup cornstarch
- 1 teaspoon vanilla extract
- 1 Basic Pie Dough (see the preceding recipe) or store-bought pie dough

Directions:

1. In a medium saucepan, place the cherries and lemon juice and cook over medium heat for 10 minutes, or until the cherries begin to break down.

2. In a small bowl, stir together the sugar and cornstarch. Pour the sugar mixture into the cherries, stirring constantly. Cook the cherry mixture over low heat for 2 to 3 minutes, or until thickened. Remove from the heat and stir in the vanilla extract. Allow the cherry mixture to cool to room temperature, about 30 minutes.

3. Meanwhile, bring the pie dough to room temperature. Divide the dough into 8 equal pieces. Roll out the dough to ¼-inch thickness in circles. Place ¼ cup filling in the center of each rolled dough. Fold the dough to create a half-circle. Using a fork, press around the edges to seal the hand pies. Pierce the top

of the pie with a fork for steam release while cooking. Continue until 8 hand pies are formed.
4. Preheat the air fryer to 350°F.
5. Place a single layer of hand pies in the air fryer basket and spray with cooking spray. Cook for 8 to 10 minutes or until golden brown and cooked through.

Easy Bread Pudding

Servings: 4 | Cooking Time: 25 Minutes

Ingredients:

- 2 cups sandwich bread cubes
- ½ cup pecan pieces
- ½ cup raisins
- 3 eggs
- ¼ cup half-and-half
- ¼ cup dark corn syrup
- 1 tsp vanilla extract
- 2 tbsp bourbon
- 2 tbsp dark brown sugar
- ¼ tsp ground cinnamon
- ½ tsp nutmeg
- ¼ tsp salt

Directions:

1. Preheat air fryer at 325°F. Spread the bread pieces in a cake pan and layer pecan pieces and raisins over the top. Whisk the eggs, half-and-half, corn syrup, bourbon, vanilla extract, sugar, cinnamon, nutmeg, and salt in a bowl. Pour egg mixture over pecan pieces. Let sit for 10 minutes. Place the cake pan in the frying basket and Bake for 15 minutes. Let cool onto a cooling rack for 10 minutes before slicing. Serve immediately.

Dark Chocolate Cream Galette

Servings: 4 | Cooking Time: 55 Minutes + Cooling Time

Ingredients:

- 16 oz cream cheese, softened
- 1 cup crumbled graham crackers
- 1 cup dark cocoa powder
- ½ cup white sugar
- 1 tsp peppermint extract
- 1 tsp ground cinnamon
- 1 egg
- 1 cup condensed milk
- 2 tbsp muscovado sugar
- 1 ½ tsp butter, melted

Directions:

1. Preheat air fryer to 350°F. Place the crumbled graham crackers in a large bowl and stir in the muscovado sugar and melted butter. Spread the mixture into a greased pie pan, pressing down to form the galette base. Place the pan into the air fryer and Bake for 5 minutes. Remove the pan and set aside.
2. Place the cocoa powder, cream cheese, peppermint extract, white sugar, cinnamon, condensed milk, and egg in a large bowl and whip thoroughly to combine. Spoon the chocolate mixture over the graham cracker crust and level the top with a spatula. Put in the air fryer and Bake for 40 minutes until firm. Transfer the cookies to a wire rack to cool. Serve and enjoy!

Strawberry Donut Bites

Servings: 6 | Cooking Time: 25 Minutes

Ingredients:

- 2/3 cup flour
- A pinch of salt
- ½ tsp baking powder
- 1 tsp vanilla extract
- 2 tbsp light brown sugar
- 1 tbsp honey
- ½ cup diced strawberries
- 1 tbsp butter, melted
- 2 tbsp powdered sugar
- 2 tsp sour cream
- ¼ cup crushed pretzels

Directions:

1. Preheat air fryer at 325°F. In a bowl, sift flour, baking powder, and salt. Add in vanilla, brown sugar, honey, 2 tbsp of water, butter, and strawberries and whisk until combined. Form dough into balls. Place the balls on a lightly greased pizza pan, place them in the frying basket, and Air Fry for 10-12 minutes. Let cool onto a cooling rack for 5 minutes. Mix the powdered sugar and sour cream in a small bowl, 1 tsp of sour cream at a time until you reach your desired consistency. Gently pour over the donut bites. Scatter with crushed pretzels and serve.

Coconut Rice Cake

Servings: 8 | Cooking Time: 30 Minutes

Ingredients:

- 1 cup all-natural coconut water
- 1 cup unsweetened coconut milk
- 1 teaspoon almond extract
- ¼ teaspoon salt
- 4 tablespoons honey
- cooking spray
- ¾ cup raw jasmine rice
- 2 cups sliced or cubed fruit

Directions:

1. In a medium bowl, mix together the coconut water, coconut milk, almond extract, salt, and honey.
2. Spray air fryer baking pan with cooking spray and add the rice.
3. Pour liquid mixture over rice.
4. Cook at 360°F for 15minutes. Stir and cook for 15 minutes longer or until rice grains are tender.
5. Allow cake to cool slightly. Run a dull knife around edge of cake, inside the pan. Turn the cake out onto a platter and garnish with fruit.

Oreo-coated Peanut Butter Cups

Servings:8 | Cooking Time: 4 Minutes

Ingredients:

- 8 Standard ¾-ounce peanut butter cups, frozen
- ⅓ cup All-purpose flour
- 2 Large egg white(s), beaten until foamy
- 16 Oreos or other creme-filled chocolate sandwich cookies, ground to crumbs in a food processor
- Vegetable oil spray

Directions:

1. Set up and fill three shallow soup plates or small pie plates on your counter: one for the flour, one for the beaten egg white(s), and one for the cookie crumbs.
2. Dip a frozen peanut butter cup in the flour, turning it to coat all sides. Shake off any excess, then set it in the beaten egg white(s). Turn it to coat all sides, then let any excess egg white slip back into the rest. Set the candy bar in the cookie crumbs. Turn to coat on all parts, even the sides. Dip the peanut butter cup back in the egg white(s) as before, then into the cookie crumbs as before, making sure you have a solid, even coating all around the cup. Set aside while you dip and coat the remaining cups.
3. When all the peanut butter cups are dipped and coated, lightly coat them on all sides with the vegetable oil spray. Set them on a plate and freeze while the air fryer heats.
4. Preheat the air fryer to 400°F.
5. Set the dipped cups wider side up in the basket with as much air space between them as possible. Air-fry undisturbed for 4 minutes, or until they feel soft but the coating is set.
6. Turn off the machine and remove the basket from it. Set aside the basket with the fried cups for 10 minutes. Use a nonstick-safe spatula to transfer the fried cups to a wire rack. Cool for at least another 5 minutes before serving.

Healthy Chickpea Cookies

Servings: 6 | Cooking Time: 25 Minutes

Ingredients:

- 1 cup canned chickpeas
- 2 tsp vanilla extract
- 1 tsp lemon juice
- 1/3 cup date paste
- 2 tbsp butter, melted
- 1/3 cup flour
- ½ tsp baking powder
- ¼ cup dark chocolate chips

Directions:

1. Preheat air fryer to 320°F. Line the basket with parchment paper. In a blender, blitz chickpeas, vanilla extract, and lemon juice until smooth. Remove it to a bowl. Stir in date paste and butter until well combined. Then mix in flour, baking powder, chocolate chips. Make 2-tablespoon balls out of the mixture. Place the balls onto the paper, flatten them into a cookie shape. Bake for 13 minutes until golden brown. Let cool slightly. Serve.

Banana Bread Cake

Servings: 6 | Cooking Time: 18-22 Minutes

Ingredients:

- ¾ cup plus 2 tablespoons All-purpose flour
- ½ teaspoon Baking powder
- ¼ teaspoon Baking soda
- ¼ teaspoon Table salt
- 4 tablespoons (¼ cup/½ stick) Butter, at room temperature
- ½ cup Granulated white sugar
- 2 Small ripe bananas, peeled
- 5 tablespoons Pasteurized egg substitute, such as Egg Beaters
- ¼ cup Buttermilk
- ¾ teaspoon Vanilla extract
- Baking spray (see here)

Directions:

1. Preheat the air fryer to 325°F (or 330°F, if that's the closest setting).
2. Mix the flour, baking powder, baking soda, and salt in a small bowl until well combined.
3. Using an electric hand mixer at medium speed, beat the butter and sugar in a medium bowl until creamy and smooth, about 3 minutes, occasionally scraping down the inside of the bowl.
4. Beat in the bananas until smooth. Then beat in egg substitute or egg, buttermilk, and vanilla until uniform. (The batter may look curdled at this stage. The flour mixture will smooth it out.) Add the flour mixture and beat at low speed until smooth and creamy.
5. Use the baking spray to generously coat the inside of a 6-inch round cake pan for a small batch, a 7-inch round cake pan for a medium batch, or an 8-inch round cake pan for a large batch. Scrape and spread the batter into the pan, smoothing the batter out to an even layer.
6. Set the pan in the basket and air-fry for 18 minutes for a 6-inch layer, 20 minutes for a 7-inch layer, or 22 minutes for an 8-inch layer, or until the cake is well browned and set even if there's a little soft give right at the center. Start checking it at the 16-minute mark to know where you are.
7. Use hot pads or silicone baking mitts to transfer the cake pan to a wire rack. To unmold, set a cutting board over the baking pan and invert both the board and the pan. Lift the still-warm pan off the cake layer. Set the wire rack on top of that layer and invert all of it with the cutting board so that the cake layer is now right side up on the wire rack. Remove the cutting board and continue cooling the cake for at least 10 minutes or to room temperature, about 40 minutes, before slicing into wedges.

Keto Cheesecake Cups

Servings: 6 | Cooking Time: 10 Minutes

Ingredients:

- 8 ounces cream cheese
- ¼ cup plain whole-milk Greek yogurt
- 1 large egg
- 1 teaspoon pure vanilla extract
- 3 tablespoons monk fruit sweetener
- ¼ teaspoon salt
- ½ cup walnuts, roughly chopped

Directions:

1. Preheat the air fryer to 315°F.
2. In a large bowl, use a hand mixer to beat the cream cheese together with the yogurt, egg, vanilla, sweetener, and salt. When combined, fold in the chopped walnuts.
3. Set 6 silicone muffin liners inside an air-fryer-safe pan. Note: This is to allow for an easier time getting the cheesecake bites in and out. If you don't have a pan, you can place them directly in the air fryer basket.
4. Evenly fill the cupcake liners with cheesecake batter.
5. Carefully place the pan into the air fryer basket and cook for about 10 minutes, or until the tops are lightly browned and firm.
6. Carefully remove the pan when done and place in the refrigerator for 3 hours to firm up before serving.

Brownies After Dark

Servings: 4 | Cooking Time: 13 Minutes

Ingredients:

- 1 egg
- ½ cup granulated sugar
- ¼ teaspoon salt
- ½ teaspoon vanilla
- ¼ cup butter, melted
- ¼ cup flour, plus 2 tablespoons
- ¼ cup cocoa
- cooking spray
- Optional
- vanilla ice cream
- caramel sauce
- whipped cream

Directions:

1. Beat together egg, sugar, salt, and vanilla until light.
2. Add melted butter and mix well.
3. Stir in flour and cocoa.
4. Spray 6 x 6-inch baking pan lightly with cooking spray.
5. Spread batter in pan and cook at 330°F for 13 minutes. Cool and cut into 4 large squares or 16 small brownie bites.

Pecan-oat Filled Apples

Servings: 4 | Cooking Time: 20 Minutes

Ingredients:

- 2 cored Granny Smith apples, halved
- ¼ cup rolled oats
- 2 tbsp honey
- ½ tsp ground cinnamon
- ½ tsp ground ginger
- 2 tbsp chopped pecans
- A pinch of salt
- 1 tbsp olive oil

Directions:

1. Preheat air fryer to 380°F. Combine together the oats, honey, cinnamon, ginger, pecans, salt, and olive oil in a bowl. Scoop a quarter of the oat mixture onto the top of each half apple. Put the apples in the frying basket and Roast for 12-15 minutes until the apples are fork-tender.

Black And Blue Clafoutis

Servings: 2 | Cooking Time: 15minutes

Ingredients:

- 6-inch pie pan
- 3 large eggs
- ½ cup sugar
- 1 teaspoon vanilla extract
- 2 tablespoons butter, melted 1 cup milk
- ½ cup all-purpose flour*
- 1 cup blackberries
- 1 cup blueberries
- 2 tablespoons confectioners' sugar

Directions:

1. Preheat the air fryer to 320°F.
2. Combine the eggs and sugar in a bowl and whisk vigorously until smooth, lighter in color and well combined. Add the vanilla extract, butter and milk and whisk together well. Add the flour and whisk just until no lumps or streaks of white remain.
3. Scatter half the blueberries and blackberries in a greased (6-inch) pie pan or cake pan. Pour half of the batter (about 1¼ cups) on top of the berries and transfer the tart pan to the air fryer basket. You can use an aluminum foil sling to help with this by taking a long piece of aluminum foil, folding it in half lengthwise twice until it is roughly 26-inches by 3-inches. Place this under the pie dish and hold the ends of the foil to move the pie dish in and out of the air fryer basket. Tuck the ends of the foil beside the pie dish while it cooks in the air fryer.
4. Air-fry at 320°F for 15 minutes or until the clafoutis has puffed up and is still a little jiggly in the center. Remove the clafoutis from the air fryer, invert it onto a plate and let it cool while you bake the second batch. Serve the clafoutis warm, dusted with confectioners' sugar on top.

Giant Buttery Chocolate Chip Cookie

Servings: 4 | Cooking Time: 16 Minutes

Ingredients:

- ⅔ cup plus 1 tablespoon All-purpose flour
- ¼ teaspoon Baking soda
- ¼ teaspoon Table salt
- Baking spray (see the headnote)
- 4 tablespoons (¼ cup/½ stick) plus 1 teaspoon Butter, at room temperature
- ¼ cup plus 1 teaspoon Packed dark brown sugar
- 3 tablespoons plus 1 teaspoon Granulated white sugar
- 2½ tablespoons Pasteurized egg substitute, such as Egg Beaters
- ½ teaspoon Vanilla extract
- ¾ cup plus 1 tablespoon Semisweet or bittersweet chocolate chips

Directions:

1. Preheat the air fryer to 350°F .
2. Whisk the flour, baking soda, and salt in a bowl until well combined.
3. For a small air fryer, coat the inside of a 6-inch round cake pan with baking spray. For a medium air fryer, coat the inside of a 7-inch round cake pan with baking spray. And for a large air fryer, coat the inside of an 8-inch round cake pan with baking spray.
4. Using a hand electric mixer at medium speed, beat the butter, brown sugar, and granulated white sugar

in a bowl until smooth and thick, about 3 minutes, scraping down the inside of the bowl several times.

5. Beat in the pasteurized egg substitute or egg (as applicable) and vanilla until uniform. Scrape down and remove the beaters. Fold in the flour mixture and chocolate chips with a rubber spatula, just until combined. Scrape and gently press this dough into the prepared pan, getting it even across the pan to the perimeter.

6. Set the pan in the basket and air-fry undisturbed for 16 minutes, or until the cookie is puffed, browned, and feels set to the touch.

7. Transfer the pan to a wire rack and cool for 10 minutes. Loosen the cookie from the perimeter with a spatula, then invert the pan onto a cutting board and let the cookie come free. Remove the pan and reinvert the cookie onto the wire rack. Cool for 5 minutes more before slicing into wedges to serve.

Fried Oreos

Servings: 12 | Cooking Time: 6 Minutes Per Batch

Ingredients:

- oil for misting or nonstick spray
- 1 cup complete pancake and waffle mix
- 1 teaspoon vanilla extract
- ½ cup water, plus 2 tablespoons
- 12 Oreos or other chocolate sandwich cookies
- 1 tablespoon confectioners' sugar

Directions:

1. Spray baking pan with oil or nonstick spray and place in basket.
2. Preheat air fryer to 390°F.
3. In a medium bowl, mix together the pancake mix, vanilla, and water.
4. Dip 4 cookies in batter and place in baking pan.
5. Cook for 6minutes, until browned.
6. Repeat steps 4 and 5 for the remaining cookies.
7. Sift sugar over warm cookies.

Cheese Blintzes

Servings: 6 | Cooking Time: 10 Minutes

Ingredients:

- 1½ 7½-ounce package(s) farmer cheese
- 3 tablespoons Regular or low-fat cream cheese (not fat-free)
- 3 tablespoons Granulated white sugar
- ¼ teaspoon Vanilla extract
- 6 Egg roll wrappers
- 3 tablespoons Butter, melted and cooled

Directions:

1. Preheat the air fryer to 375°F .
2. Use a flatware fork to mash the farmer cheese, cream cheese, sugar, and vanilla in a small bowl until smooth.
3. Set one egg roll wrapper on a clean, dry work surface. Place ¼ cup of the filling at the edge closest to you, leaving a ½-inch gap before the edge of the wrapper. Dip your clean finger in water and wet the edges of the wrapper. Fold the perpendicular sides over the filling, then roll the wrapper closed with the filling inside. Set it aside seam side down and continue filling the remainder of the wrappers.
4. Brush the wrappers on all sides with the melted butter. Be generous. Set them seam side down in the basket with as much space between them as possible. Air-fry undisturbed for 10 minutes, or until lightly browned.
5. Use a nonstick-safe spatula to transfer the blintzes to a wire rack. Cool for at least 5 minutes or up to 20 minutes before serving.

Lemon Pound Cake Bites

Servings: 6 | Cooking Time: 20 Minutes

Ingredients:

- 1 pound cake, cubed
- 1/3 cup cinnamon sugar
- ½ stick butter, melted
- 1 cup vanilla yogurt
- 3 tbsp brown sugar
- 1 tsp lemon zest

Directions:

1. Preheat the air fryer to 350°F. Drizzle the cake cubes with melted butter, then put them in the cinnamon sugar and toss until coated. Put them in a single layer in the frying basket and Air Fry for 4 minutes or until golden. Remove and place on a serving plate. Combine the yogurt, brown sugar, and lemon zest in a bowl. Serve with the cake bites.

Peach Cobbler

Servings: 4 | Cooking Time: 12 Minutes

Ingredients:

- 16 ounces frozen peaches, thawed, with juice (do not drain)
- 6 tablespoons sugar
- 1 tablespoon cornstarch
- 1 tablespoon water
- Crust
- ½ cup flour
- ¼ teaspoon salt
- 3 tablespoons butter
- 1½ tablespoons cold water
- ¼ teaspoon sugar

Directions:

1. Place peaches, including juice, and sugar in air fryer baking pan. Stir to mix well.
2. In a small cup, dissolve cornstarch in the water. Stir into peaches.
3. In a medium bowl, combine the flour and salt. Cut in butter using knives or a pastry blender. Stir in the cold water to make a stiff dough.
4. On a floured board or wax paper, pat dough into a square or circle slightly smaller than your air fryer baking pan. Cut diagonally into 4 pieces.
5. Place dough pieces on top of peaches, leaving a tiny bit of space between the edges. Sprinkle very lightly with sugar, no more than about ¼ teaspoon.
6. Cook at 360°F for 12 minutes, until fruit bubbles and crust browns.

Beef ,pork & Lamb Recipes

Easy Tex-mex Chimichangas

Servings: 2 | Cooking Time: 8 Minutes

Ingredients:

- ¼ pound Thinly sliced deli roast beef, chopped
- ½ cup (about 2 ounces) Shredded Cheddar cheese or shredded Tex-Mex cheese blend
- ¼ cup Jarred salsa verde or salsa rojo
- ½ teaspoon Ground cumin
- ½ teaspoon Dried oregano
- 2 Burrito-size (12-inch) flour tortilla(s), not corn tortillas (gluten-free, if a concern)
- ⅔ cup Canned refried beans
- Vegetable oil spray

Directions:

1. Preheat the air fryer to 375°F .
2. Stir the roast beef, cheese, salsa, cumin, and oregano in a bowl until well mixed.
3. Lay a tortilla on a clean, dry work surface. Spread ⅓ cup of the refried beans in the center lower third of the tortilla(s), leaving an inch on either side of the spread beans.
4. For one chimichanga, spread all of the roast beef mixture on top of the beans. For two, spread half of the roast beef mixture on each tortilla.
5. At either "end" of the filling mixture, fold the sides of the tortilla up and over the filling, partially covering it. Starting with the unfolded side of the tortilla just below the filling, roll the tortilla closed. Fold and roll the second filled tortilla, as necessary.
6. Coat the exterior of the tortilla(s) with vegetable oil spray. Set the chimichanga(s) seam side down in the basket, with at least ½ inch air space between them if you're working with two. Air-fry undisturbed for 8 minutes, or until the tortilla is lightly browned and crisp.
7. Use kitchen tongs to gently transfer the chimichanga(s) to a wire rack. Cool for at last 5 minutes or up to 20 minutes before serving.

Skirt Steak Fajitas

Servings: 4 | Cooking Time: 30 Minutes

Ingredients:

- 2 tablespoons olive oil
- ¼ cup lime juice
- 1 clove garlic, minced
- ½ teaspoon ground cumin
- ½ teaspoon hot sauce
- ½ teaspoon salt
- 2 tablespoons chopped fresh cilantro
- 1 pound skirt steak
- 1 onion, sliced
- 1 teaspoon chili powder
- 1 red pepper, sliced
- 1 green pepper, sliced
- salt and freshly ground black pepper
- 8 flour tortillas
- shredded lettuce, crumbled Queso Fresco (or grated Cheddar cheese), sliced black olives, diced tomatoes, sour cream and guacamole for serving

Directions:

1. Combine the olive oil, lime juice, garlic, cumin, hot sauce, salt and cilantro in a shallow dish. Add the skirt steak and turn it over several times to coat all sides. Pierce the steak with a needle-style meat tenderizer or paring knife. Marinate the steak in the refrigerator for at least 3 hours, or overnight. When you are ready to cook, remove the steak from the refrigerator and let it sit at room temperature for 30 minutes.
2. Preheat the air fryer to 400°F.
3. Toss the onion slices with the chili powder and a little olive oil and transfer them to the air fryer basket. Air-fry at 400°F for 5 minutes. Add the red and green peppers to the air fryer basket with the onions, season with salt and pepper and air-fry for 8 more minutes, until the onions and peppers are soft. Transfer the vegetables to a dish and cover with aluminum foil to keep warm.
4. Place the skirt steak in the air fryer basket and pour the marinade over the top. Air-fry at 400°F for 12 minutes. Flip the steak over and air-fry at 400°F for an additional 5 minutes. (The time needed for your steak will depend on the thickness of the skirt steak. 17 minutes should bring your steak to roughly medium.) Transfer the cooked steak to a cutting board and let the

steak rest for a few minutes. If the peppers and onions need to be heated, return them to the air fryer for just 1 to 2 minutes.
5. Thinly slice the steak at an angle, cutting against the grain of the steak. Serve the steak with the onions and peppers, the warm tortillas and the fajita toppings on the side so that everyone can make their own fajita.

Mushroom & Quinoa-stuffed Pork Loins

Servings: 3 | Cooking Time: 25 Minutes

Ingredients:

- 3 boneless center-cut pork loins, pocket cut in each loin
- ½ cup diced white mushrooms
- 1 tsp vegetable oil
- 3 bacon slices, diced
- ½ onion, peeled and diced
- 1 cup baby spinach
- Salt and pepper to taste
- ½ cup cooked quinoa
- ½ cup mozzarella cheese

Directions:

1. Warm the oil in a skillet over medium heat. Add the bacon and cook for 3 minutes until the fat is rendered but not crispy. Add in onion and mushrooms and stir-fry for 3 minutes until the onions are translucent. Stir in spinach, salt, and pepper and cook for 1 minute until the spinach wilts. Set aside and toss in quinoa.
2. Preheat air fryer at 350°F. Stuff quinoa mixture into each pork loin and sprinkle with mozzarella cheese. Place them in the frying basket and Air Fry for 11 minutes. Let rest onto a cutting board for 5 minutes before serving.

Indian Fry Bread Tacos

Servings: 4 | Cooking Time: 20 Minutes

Ingredients:

- 1 cup all-purpose flour
- 1½ teaspoons salt, divided
- 1½ teaspoons baking powder
- ¼ cup milk
- ¼ cup warm water
- ½ pound lean ground beef
- One 14.5-ounce can pinto beans, drained and rinsed
- 1 tablespoon taco seasoning
- ½ cup shredded cheddar cheese
- 2 cups shredded lettuce
- ¼ cup black olives, chopped
- 1 Roma tomato, diced
- 1 avocado, diced
- 1 lime

Directions:

1. In a large bowl, whisk together the flour, 1 teaspoon of the salt, and baking powder. Make a well in the center and add in the milk and water. Form a ball and gently knead the dough four times. Cover the bowl with a damp towel, and set aside.
2. Preheat the air fryer to 380°F.
3. In a medium bowl, mix together the ground beef, beans, and taco seasoning. Crumble the meat mixture into the air fryer basket and cook for 5 minutes; toss the meat and cook an additional 2 to 3 minutes, or until cooked fully. Place the cooked meat in a bowl for taco assembly; season with the remaining ½ teaspoon salt as desired.
4. On a floured surface, place the dough. Cut the dough into 4 equal parts. Using a rolling pin, roll out each piece of dough to 5 inches in diameter. Spray the dough with cooking spray and place in the air fryer basket, working in batches as needed. Cook for 3 minutes, flip over, spray with cooking spray, and cook for an additional 1 to 3 minutes, until golden and puffy.
5. To assemble, place the fry breads on a serving platter. Equally divide the meat and bean mixture on top of the fry bread. Divide the cheese, lettuce, olives, tomatoes, and avocado among the four tacos. Squeeze lime over the top prior to serving.

Beef Short Ribs

Servings: 4 | Cooking Time: 20 Minutes

Ingredients:

- 2 tablespoons soy sauce
- 1 tablespoon sesame oil
- 2 tablespoons brown sugar
- 1 teaspoon ground ginger
- 2 garlic cloves, crushed
- 1 pound beef short ribs

Directions:

1. In a small bowl, mix together the soy sauce, sesame oil, brown sugar, and ginger. Transfer the mixture to a large resealable plastic bag, and place the garlic cloves and short ribs into the bag. Secure and place in the refrigerator for an hour (or overnight).
2. When you're ready to prepare the dish, preheat the

air fryer to 330°F.

3. Liberally spray the air fryer basket with olive oil mist and set the beef short ribs in the basket.

4. Cook for 10 minutes, flip the short ribs, and then cook another 10 minutes.

5. Remove the short ribs from the air fryer basket, loosely cover with aluminum foil, and let them rest. The short ribs will continue to cook after they're removed from the basket. Check the internal temperature after 5 minutes to make sure it reached 145°F if you prefer a well-done meat. If it didn't reach 145°F and you would like it to be cooked longer, you can put it back into the air fryer basket at 330°F for another 3 minutes.

6. Remove from the basket and let it rest, covered with aluminum foil, for 5 minutes. Serve immediately.

Perfect Strip Steaks

Servings: 2 | Cooking Time: 17 Minutes

Ingredients:

- 1½ tablespoons Olive oil
- 1½ tablespoons Minced garlic
- 2 teaspoons Ground black pepper
- 1 teaspoon Table salt
- 2 ¾-pound boneless beef strip steak(s)

Directions:

1. Preheat the air fryer to 375°F (or 380°F or 390°F, if one of these is the closest setting).

2. Mix the oil, garlic, pepper, and salt in a small bowl, then smear this mixture over both sides of the steak(s).

3. When the machine is at temperature, put the steak(s) in the basket with as much air space as possible between them for the larger batch. They should not overlap or even touch. That said, even just a ¼-inch between them will work. Air-fry for 12 minutes, turning once, until an instant-read meat thermometer inserted into the thickest part of a steak registers 127°F for rare (not USDA-approved). Or air-fry for 15 minutes, turning once, until an instant-read meat thermometer registers 145°F for medium (USDA-approved). If the machine is at 390°F, the steaks may cook 2 minutes more quickly than the stated timing.

4. Use kitchen tongs to transfer the steak(s) to a wire rack. Cool for 5 minutes before serving.

Calzones South Of The Border

Servings: 8 | Cooking Time: 8 Minutes

Ingredients:

- Filling
- ¼ pound ground pork sausage
- ½ teaspoon chile powder
- ¼ teaspoon ground cumin
- ⅛ teaspoon garlic powder
- ⅛ teaspoon onion powder
- ⅛ teaspoon oregano
- ½ cup ricotta cheese
- 1 ounce sharp Cheddar cheese, shredded
- 2 ounces Pepper Jack cheese, shredded
- 1 4-ounce can chopped green chiles, drained
- oil for misting or cooking spray
- salsa, sour cream, or guacamole
- Crust
- 2 cups white wheat flour, plus more for kneading and rolling
- 1 package (¼ ounce) RapidRise yeast
- 1 teaspoon salt
- ½ teaspoon chile powder
- ½ teaspoon ground cumin
- 1 cup warm water (115°F to 125°F)
- 2 teaspoons olive oil

Directions:

1. Crumble sausage into air fryer baking pan and stir in the filling seasonings: chile powder, cumin, garlic powder, onion powder, and oregano. Cook at 390°F for 2minutes. Stir, breaking apart, and cook for 3 to 4minutes, until well done. Remove and set aside on paper towels to drain.

2. To make dough, combine flour, yeast, salt, chile powder, and cumin. Stir in warm water and oil until soft dough forms. Turn out onto lightly floured board and knead for 3 or 4minutes. Let dough rest for 10minutes.

3. Place the three cheeses in a medium bowl. Add cooked sausage and chiles and stir until well mixed.

4. Cut dough into 8 pieces.

5. Working with 4 pieces of the dough, press each into a circle about 5 inches in diameter. Top each dough circle with 2 heaping tablespoons of filling. Fold over into a half-moon shape and press edges together. Seal edges firmly to prevent leakage. Spray both sides with oil or cooking spray.

6. Place 4 calzones in air fryer basket and cook at 360°F for 5minutes. Mist with oil or spray and cook

for 3minutes, until crust is done and nicely browned.
7. While the first batch is cooking, press out the remaining dough, fill, and shape into calzones.
8. Spray both sides with oil or cooking spray and cook for 5minutes. If needed, mist with oil and continue cooking for 3 minutes longer. This second batch will cook a little faster than the first because your air fryer is already hot.
9. Serve plain or with salsa, sour cream, or guacamole.

Lemon-garlic Strip Steak

Servings: 2 | Cooking Time: 15 Minutes

Ingredients:

- 3 cloves garlic, minced
- 1 tbsp lemon juice
- 1 tbsp olive oil
- Salt and pepper to taste
- 1 tbsp chopped parsley
- ½ tsp chopped rosemary
- ½ tsp chopped sage
- 1 strip steak

Directions:

1. In a small bowl, whisk all ingredients. Brush mixture over strip steak and let marinate covered in the fridge for 30 minutes. Preheat air fryer at 400ºF. Place strip steak in the greased frying basket and Bake for 8 minutes until rare, turning once. Let rest onto a cutting board for 5 minutes before serving.

Natchitoches Meat Pies

Servings: 8 | Cooking Time: 12 Minutes

Ingredients:

- Filling
- ½ pound lean ground beef
- ¼ cup finely chopped onion
- ¼ cup finely chopped green bell pepper
- ⅛ teaspoon salt
- ½ teaspoon garlic powder
- ½ teaspoon red pepper flakes
- 1 tablespoon low sodium Worcestershire sauce
- Crust
- 2 cups self-rising flour
- ¼ cup butter, finely diced
- 1 cup milk
- Egg Wash
- 1 egg
- 1 tablespoon water or milk
- oil for misting or cooking spray

Directions:

1. Mix all filling ingredients well and shape into 4 small patties.
2. Cook patties in air fryer basket at 390°F for 10 to 12minutes or until well done.
3. Place patties in large bowl and use fork and knife to crumble meat into very small pieces. Set aside.
4. To make the crust, use a pastry blender or fork to cut the butter into the flour until well mixed. Add milk and stir until dough stiffens.
5. Divide dough into 8 equal portions.
6. On a lightly floured surface, roll each portion of dough into a circle. The circle should be thin and about 5 inches in diameter, but don't worry about getting a perfect shape. Uneven circles result in a rustic look that many people prefer.
7. Spoon 2 tablespoons of meat filling onto each dough circle.
8. Brush egg wash all the way around the edge of dough circle, about ½-inch deep.
9. Fold each circle in half and press dough with tines of a dinner fork to seal the edges all the way around.
10. Brush tops of sealed meat pies with egg wash.
11. Cook filled pies in a single layer in air fryer basket at 360°F for 4minutes. Spray tops with oil or cooking spray, turn pies over, and spray bottoms with oil or cooking spray. Cook for an additional 2minutes.
12. Repeat previous step to cook remaining pies.

Crispy Ham And Eggs

Servings: 3 | Cooking Time: 9 Minutes

Ingredients:

- 2 cups Rice-puff cereal, such as Rice Krispies
- ¼ cup Maple syrup
- ½ pound ¼- to ½-inch-thick ham steak (gluten-free, if a concern)
- 1 tablespoon Unsalted butter
- 3 Large eggs
- ⅛ teaspoon Table salt
- ⅛ teaspoon Ground black pepper

Directions:

1. Preheat the air fryer to 400°F.
2. Pour the cereal into a food processor, cover, and process until finely ground. Pour the ground cereal into a shallow soup plate or a small pie plate.
3. Smear the maple syrup on both sides of the ham, then set the ham into the ground cereal. Turn a few

times, pressing gently, until evenly coated.

4. Set the ham steak in the basket and air-fry undisturbed for 5 minutes, or until browned.

5. Meanwhile, melt the butter in a medium or large nonstick skillet set over medium heat. Crack the eggs into the skillet and cook until the whites are set and the yolks are hot, about 3 minutes (or 4 minutes for a more set yolk.) Season with the salt and pepper.

6. When the ham is ready, transfer it to a serving platter, then slip the eggs from the skillet on top of it. Divide into portions to serve.

Country-style Pork Ribs

Servings: 4 | Cooking Time: 30 Minutes

Ingredients:

- 2 tbsp cornstarch
- 2 tbsp olive oil
- 1 tsp mustard powder
- ½ tsp thyme
- ½ tsp garlic powder
- 1 tsp paprika
- Salt and pepper to taste
- 12 country-style pork ribs

Directions:

1. Preheat air fryer to 400°F. Mix together cornstarch, olive oil, mustard powder, thyme, garlic powder, paprika, salt, and pepper in a bowl. Rub the seasoned mixture onto the ribs. Put the ribs into the frying basket. Bake for 14-16 minutes, flipping once until the ribs are crisp. Serve.

Greek Pork Chops

Servings: 4 | Cooking Time: 30 Minutes

Ingredients:

- 3 tbsp grated Halloumi cheese
- 4 pork chops
- 1 tsp Greek seasoning
- Salt and pepper to taste
- ¼ cup all-purpose flour
- 2 tbsp bread crumbs

Directions:

1. Preheat air fryer to 380°F. Season the pork chops with Greek seasoning, salt and pepper. In a shallow bowl, add flour. In another shallow bowl, combine the crumbs and Halloumi. Dip the chops in the flour, then in the bread crumbs. Place them in the fryer and spray with cooking oil. Bake for 12-14 minutes, flipping once. Serve warm.

Cinnamon-stick Kofta Skewers

Servings: 8 | Cooking Time: 15 Minutes

Ingredients:

- 1 pound Lean ground beef
- ½ teaspoon Ground cumin
- ½ teaspoon Onion powder
- ½ teaspoon Ground dried turmeric
- ½ teaspoon Ground cinnamon
- ½ teaspoon Table salt
- Up to a ⅛ teaspoon Cayenne
- 8 3½- to 4-inch-long cinnamon sticks (see the headnote)
- Vegetable oil spray

Directions:

1. Preheat the air fryer to 375°F .

2. Gently mix the ground beef, cumin, onion powder, turmeric, cinnamon, salt, and cayenne in a bowl until the meat is evenly mixed with the spices. (Clean, dry hands work best!) Divide this mixture into 2-ounce portions, each about the size of a golf ball.

3. Wrap one portion of the meat mixture around a cinnamon stick, using about three-quarters of the length of the stick, covering one end but leaving a little "handle" of cinnamon stick protruding from the other end. Set aside and continue making more kofta skewers.

4. Generously coat the formed kofta skewers on all sides with vegetable oil spray. Set them in the basket with as much air space between them as possible. Air-fry undisturbed for 13 minutes, or until browned and cooked through. If the machine is at 360°F, you may need to add 2 minutes to the cooking time.

5. Use a nonstick-safe spatula, and perhaps kitchen tongs for balance, to gently transfer the kofta skewers to a wire rack. Cool for at least 5 minutes or up to 20 minutes before serving.

Calf's Liver

Servings: 4 | Cooking Time: 5 Minutes

Ingredients:

- 1 pound sliced calf's liver
- salt and pepper
- 2 eggs
- 2 tablespoons milk
- ½ cup whole wheat flour
- 1½ cups panko breadcrumbs

- ½ cup plain breadcrumbs
- ½ teaspoon salt
- ¼ teaspoon pepper
- oil for misting or cooking spray

Directions:

1. Cut liver slices crosswise into strips about ½-inch wide. Sprinkle with salt and pepper to taste.
2. Beat together egg and milk in a shallow dish.
3. Place wheat flour in a second shallow dish.
4. In a third shallow dish, mix together panko, plain breadcrumbs, ½ teaspoon salt, and ¼ teaspoon pepper.
5. Preheat air fryer to 390°F.
6. Dip liver strips in flour, egg wash, and then breadcrumbs, pressing in coating slightly to make crumbs stick.
7. Cooking half the liver at a time, place strips in air fryer basket in a single layer, close but not touching. Cook at 390°F for 5 minutes or until done to your preference.
8. Repeat step 7 to cook remaining liver.

Pork Chops With Cereal Crust

Servings: 2 | Cooking Time: 20 Minutes

Ingredients:

- ¼ cup grated Parmesan
- 1 egg
- 1 tbsp Dijon mustard
- ¼ cup crushed bran cereal
- ¼ tsp black pepper
- ¼ tsp cumin powder
- ¼ tsp nutmeg
- 1 tsp horseradish powder
- 2 pork chops

Directions:

1. Preheat air fryer at 350ºF. Whisk egg and mustard in a bowl. In another bowl, combine Parmesan cheese, cumin powder, nutmeg, horseradish powder, bran cereal, and black pepper. Dip pork chops in the egg mixture, then dredge them in the cheese mixture. Place pork chops in the frying basket and Air Fry for 12 minutes, tossing once. Let rest onto a cutting board for 5 minutes. Serve.

Mustard-crusted Rib-eye

Servings: 2 | Cooking Time: 9 Minutes

Ingredients:

- Two 6-ounce rib-eye steaks, about 1-inch thick
- 1 teaspoon coarse salt
- ½ teaspoon coarse black pepper
- 2 tablespoons Dijon mustard

Directions:

1. Rub the steaks with the salt and pepper. Then spread the mustard on both sides of the steaks. Cover with foil and let the steaks sit at room temperature for 30 minutes.
2. Preheat the air fryer to 390°F.
3. Cook the steaks for 9 minutes. Check for an internal temperature of 140°F and immediately remove the steaks and let them rest for 5 minutes before slicing.

Rib Eye Bites With Mushrooms

Servings: 4 | Cooking Time: 30 Minutes

Ingredients:

- 1 ¼ lb boneless rib-eye or sirloin steak, cubed
- 8 oz button mushrooms, halved
- 4 tbsp rapeseed oil
- 1 onion, chopped
- 2 garlic cloves, minced
- Salt and pepper to taste
- 2 tsp lime juice
- 1 tsp dried marjoram
- 2 tbsp chopped parsley

Directions:

1. Preheat the air fryer to 400°F. Combine the rapeseed oil, onion, mushrooms, garlic, steak cubes, salt, pepper, lime juice, marjoram, and parsley in a baking pan. Put it in the frying basket and Bake for 12-15 minutes, stirring once or twice to ensure an even cooking, and until golden brown. The veggies should be tender. Serve hot.

Zesty London Broil

Servings: 4 | Cooking Time: 28 Minutes

Ingredients:

- ⅔ cup ketchup
- ¼ cup honey
- ¼ cup olive oil
- 2 tablespoons apple cider vinegar
- 2 tablespoons Worcestershire sauce

- 2 tablespoons minced onion
- ½ teaspoon paprika
- 1 teaspoon salt
- 1 teaspoon freshly ground black pepper
- 2 pounds London broil, top round or flank steak (about 1-inch thick)

Directions:

1. Combine the ketchup, honey, olive oil, apple cider vinegar, Worcestershire sauce, minced onion, paprika, salt and pepper in a small bowl and whisk together.
2. Generously pierce both sides of the meat with a fork or meat tenderizer and place it in a shallow dish. Pour the marinade mixture over the steak, making sure all sides of the meat get coated with the marinade. Cover and refrigerate overnight.
3. Preheat the air fryer to 400°F.
4. Transfer the London broil to the air fryer basket and air-fry for 28 minutes, depending on how rare or well done you like your steak. Flip the steak over halfway through the cooking time.
5. Remove the London broil from the air fryer and let it rest for five minutes on a cutting board. To serve, thinly slice the meat against the grain and transfer to a serving platter.

Minted Lamb Chops

Servings: 4 | Cooking Time: 20 Minutes

Ingredients:

- 8 lamb chops
- 2 tsp olive oil
- 1 ½ tsp chopped mint leaves
- 1 tsp ground coriander
- 1 lemon, zested
- ½ tsp baharat seasoning
- 1 garlic clove, minced
- Salt and pepper to taste

Directions:

1. Preheat air fryer to 390°F. Coat the lamb chops with olive oil. Set aside. Mix mint, coriander, baharat, zest, garlic, salt and pepper in a bowl. Rub the seasoning onto both sides of the chops. Place the chops in the greased frying basket and Air Fry for 10 minutes. Flip the lamb chops and cook for another 5 minutes. Let the lamb chops rest for a few minutes. Serve right away.

Blossom Bbq Pork Chops

Servings: 2 | Cooking Time: 20 Minutes

Ingredients:

- 2 tbsp cherry preserves
- 1 tbsp honey
- 1 tbsp Dijon mustard
- 2 tsp light brown sugar
- 1 tsp Worcestershire sauce
- 1 tbsp lime juice
- 1 tbsp olive oil
- 2 cloves garlic, minced
- 1 tbsp chopped parsley
- 2 pork chops

Directions:

1. Mix all ingredients in a bowl. Toss in pork chops. Let marinate covered in the fridge for 30 minutes.
2. Preheat air fryer at 350ºF. Place pork chops in the greased frying basket and Air Fry for 12 minutes, turning once. Let rest onto a cutting board for 5 minutes. Serve.

City "chicken"

Servings: 3 | Cooking Time: 10 Minutes

Ingredients:

- 1 pound Pork tenderloin, cut into 2-inch cubes
- ½ cup All-purpose flour or tapioca flour
- 1 Large egg(s)
- 1 teaspoon Dried poultry seasoning blend
- 1¼ cups Plain panko bread crumbs (gluten-free, if a concern)
- Vegetable oil spray

Directions:

1. Preheat the air fryer to 350°F .
2. Thread 3 or 4 pieces of pork on a 4-inch bamboo skewer. You'll need 2 or 3 skewers for a small batch, 3 or 4 for a medium, and up to 6 for a large batch.
3. Set up and fill three shallow soup plates or small pie plates on your counter: one for the flour; one for the egg(s), beaten with the poultry seasoning until foamy; and one for the bread crumbs.
4. Dip and roll one skewer into the flour, coating all sides of the meat. Gently shake off any excess flour, then dip and roll the skewer in the egg mixture. Let any excess egg mixture slip back into the rest, then set the skewer in the bread crumbs and roll it around, pressing gently, until the exterior surfaces of the meat are evenly coated. Generously coat the meat on the

skewer with vegetable oil spray. Set aside and continue dredging, dipping, coating, and spraying the remaining skewers.
5. Set the skewers in the basket in one layer and air-fry undisturbed for 10 minutes, or until brown and crunchy.
6. Use kitchen tongs to transfer the skewers to a wire rack. Cool for a minute or two before serving.

Delicious Juicy Pork Meatballs

Servings:4 | Cooking Time: 35 Minutes

Ingredients:

- ¼ cup grated cheddar cheese
- 1 lb ground pork
- 1 egg
- 1 tbsp Greek yogurt
- ½ tsp onion powder
- ¼ cup chopped parsley
- 2 tbsp bread crumbs
- ¼ tsp garlic powder
- Salt and pepper to taste

Directions:

1. Preheat air fryer to 350ºF. In a bowl, combine the ground pork, egg, yogurt, onion, parsley, cheddar cheese, bread crumbs, garlic, salt, and black pepper. Form mixture into 16 meatballs. Place meatballs in the lightly greased frying basket and Air Fry for 8-10 minutes, flipping once. Serve.

Rib Eye Cheesesteaks With Fried Onions

Servings: 2 | Cooking Time: 20 Minutes

Ingredients:

- 1 (12-ounce) rib eye steak
- 2 tablespoons Worcestershire sauce
- salt and freshly ground black pepper
- ½ onion, sliced
- 2 tablespoons butter, melted
- 4 ounces sliced Cheddar or provolone cheese
- 2 long hoagie rolls, lightly toasted

Directions:

1. Place the steak in the freezer for 30 minutes to make it easier to slice. When it is well-chilled, thinly slice the steak against the grain and transfer it to a bowl. Pour the Worcestershire sauce over the steak and season it with salt and pepper. Allow the meat to come to room temperature.
2. Preheat the air fryer to 400°F.
3. Toss the sliced onion with the butter and transfer it to the air fryer basket. Air-fry at 400°F for 12 minutes, shaking the basket a few times during the cooking process. Place the steak on top of the onions and air-fry for another 6 minutes, stirring the meat and onions together halfway through the cooking time.
4. When the air fryer has finished cooking, divide the steak and onions in half in the air fryer basket, pushing each half to one side of the air fryer basket. Place the cheese on top of each half, push the drawer back into the turned off air fryer and let it sit for 2 minutes, until the cheese has melted.
5. Transfer each half of the cheesesteak mixture into a toasted roll with the cheese side up and dig in!

Kielbasa Chunks With Pineapple & Peppers

Servings: 2 | Cooking Time: 10 Minutes

Ingredients:

- ¾ pound kielbasa sausage
- 1 cup bell pepper chunks (any color)
- 1 8-ounce can pineapple chunks in juice, drained
- 1 tablespoon barbeque seasoning
- 1 tablespoon soy sauce
- cooking spray

Directions:

1. Cut sausage into ½-inch slices.
2. In a medium bowl, toss all ingredients together.
3. Spray air fryer basket with nonstick cooking spray.
4. Pour sausage mixture into the basket.
5. Cook at 390°F for approximately 5minutes. Shake basket and cook an additional 5minutes.

Bbq Back Ribs

Servings: 4 | Cooking Time: 40 Minutes

Ingredients:

- 2 tbsp light brown sugar
- Salt and pepper to taste
- 2 tsp onion powder
- 1 tsp garlic powder
- 1 tsp mustard powder
- 1 tsp dried marjoram
- ½ tsp smoked paprika
- 1 tsp cayenne pepper
- 1 ½ pounds baby back ribs
- 2 tbsp barbecue sauce

Directions:

1. Preheat the air fryer to 375°F. Combine the brown sugar, salt, pepper, onion and garlic powder, mustard, paprika, cayenne, and marjoram in a bowl and mix. Pour into a small glass jar. Brush the ribs with barbecue sauce and sprinkle 1 tbsp of the seasoning mix. Rub the seasoning all over the meat. Set the ribs in the greased frying basket. Bake for 25 minutes until nicely browned, flipping them once halfway through cooking. Serve hot!

Crunchy Fried Pork Loin Chops

Servings: 3 | Cooking Time: 12 Minutes

Ingredients:

- 1 cup All-purpose flour or tapioca flour
- 1 Large egg(s), well beaten
- 1½ cups Seasoned Italian-style dried bread crumbs (gluten-free, if a concern)
- 3 4- to 5-ounce boneless center-cut pork loin chops
- Vegetable oil spray

Directions:

1. Preheat the air fryer to 350°F .
2. Set up and fill three shallow soup plates or small pie plates on your counter: one for the flour, one for the beaten egg(s), and one for the bread crumbs.
3. Dredge a pork chop in the flour, coating both sides as well as around the edge. Gently shake off any excess, then dip the chop in the egg(s), again coating both sides and the edge. Let any excess egg slip back into the rest, then set the chop in the bread crumbs, turning it and pressing gently to coat well on both sides and the edge. Coat the pork chop all over with vegetable oil spray and set aside so you can dredge, coat, and spray the additional chop(s).
4. Set the chops in the basket with as much air space between them as possible. Air-fry undisturbed for 12 minutes, or until brown and crunchy and an instant-read meat thermometer inserted into the center of a chop registers 145°F.
5. Use kitchen tongs to transfer the chops to a wire rack. Cool for 5 minutes before serving.

Glazed Meatloaf

Servings: 4 | Cooking Time: 35-55 Minutes

Ingredients:

- ½ cup Seasoned Italian-style panko bread crumbs (gluten-free, if a concern)
- ¼ cup Whole or low-fat milk
- 1 pound Lean ground beef
- 1 pound Bulk mild Italian sausage meat (gluten-free, if a concern)
- 1 Large egg(s), well beaten
- 1 teaspoon Dried thyme
- 1 teaspoon Onion powder
- 1 teaspoon Garlic powder
- Vegetable oil spray
- 1 tablespoon Ketchup (gluten-free, if a concern)
- 1 tablespoon Hoisin sauce (see here; gluten-free, if a concern)
- 2 teaspoons Pickle brine, preferably from a jar of jalapeño rings (gluten-free, if a concern)

Directions:

1. Pour the bread crumbs into a large bowl, add the milk, stir gently, and soak for 10 minutes.
2. Preheat the air fryer to 350°F .
3. Add the ground beef, Italian sausage meat, egg(s), thyme, onion powder, and garlic powder to the bowl with the bread crumbs. Blend gently until well combined. (Clean, dry hands work best!) Form this mixture into an oval loaf about 2 inches tall (its length will vary depending on the amount of ingredients) but with a flat bottom. Generously coat the top, bottom, and all sides of the loaf with vegetable oil spray.
4. Use a large, nonstick-safe spatula or perhaps silicone baking mitts to transfer the loaf to the basket. Air-fry undisturbed for 30 minutes for a small meatloaf, 40 minutes for a medium one, or 50 minutes for a large, until an instant-read meat thermometer inserted into the center of the loaf registers 165°F.
5. Whisk the ketchup, hoisin, and pickle brine in a small bowl until smooth. Brush this over the top and sides of the meatloaf and continue air-frying undisturbed for 5 minutes, or until the glaze has browned a bit. Use that same spatula or those same baking mitts to transfer the meatloaf to a cutting board. Cool for 10 minutes before slicing.

French-style Steak Salad

Servings: 4 | Cooking Time: 25 Minutes

Ingredients:

- 1 cup sliced strawberries
- 4 tbsp crumbled blue cheese
- ¼ cup olive oil
- Salt and pepper to taste
- 1 flank steak
- ¼cup balsamic vinaigrette
- 1 tbsp Dijon mustard
- 2 tbsp lemon juice
- 8 cups baby arugula
- ½ red onion, sliced
- 4 tbsp pecan pieces
- 4 tbsp sunflower seeds
- 1 sliced kiwi
- 1 sliced orange

Directions:

1. In a bowl, whisk olive oil, salt, lemon juice and pepper. Toss in flank steak and let marinate covered in the fridge for 30 minutes up to overnight. Preheat air fryer at 325°F. Place flank steak in the greased frying basket and Bake for 18-20 minutes until rare, flipping once. Let rest for 5 minutes before slicing thinly against the grain.
2. In a salad bowl, whisk balsamic vinaigrette and mustard. Stir in arugula, salt, and pepper. Divide between 4 serving bowls. Top each salad with blue cheese, onion, pecan, sunflower seeds, strawberries, kiwi, orange and sliced steak. Serve immediately.

Meat Loaves

Servings: 4 | Cooking Time: 19 Minutes

Ingredients:

- Sauce
- ¼ cup white vinegar
- ¼ cup brown sugar
- 2 tablespoons Worcestershire sauce
- ½ cup ketchup
- Meat Loaves
- 1 pound very lean ground beef
- ⅔ cup dry bread (approx. 1 slice torn into small pieces)
- 1 egg
- ⅓ cup minced onion
- 1 teaspoon salt
- 2 tablespoons ketchup

Directions:

1. In a small saucepan, combine all sauce ingredients and bring to a boil. Remove from heat and stir to ensure that brown sugar dissolves completely.
2. In a large bowl, combine the beef, bread, egg, onion, salt, and ketchup. Mix well.
3. Divide meat mixture into 4 portions and shape each into a thick, round patty. Patties will be about 3 to 3½ inches in diameter, and all four should fit easily into the air fryer basket at once.
4. Cook at 360°F for 18 minutes, until meat is well done. Baste tops of mini loaves with a small amount of sauce, and cook 1 minute.
5. Serve hot with additional sauce on the side.

Chipotle Pork Meatballs

Servings:4 | Cooking Time: 35 Minutes

Ingredients:

- 1 lb ground pork
- 1 egg
- ¼ cup chipotle sauce
- ¼ cup grated celery
- ¼ cup chopped parsley
- ¼ cup chopped cilantro
- ¼ cup flour
- ¼ tsp salt

Directions:

1. Preheat air fryer to 350°F. In a large bowl, combine the ground pork, egg, chipotle sauce, celery, parsley, cilantro, flour, and salt. Form mixture into 16 meatballs. Place the meatballs in the lightly greased frying basket and Air Fry for 8-10 minutes, flipping once. Serve immediately!

Poultry Recipes

Fiery Chicken Meatballs

Servings: 4 | Cooking Time: 20 Minutes + Chilling Time

Ingredients:

- 2 jalapeños, seeded and diced
- 2 tbsp shredded Cheddar cheese
- 1 tsp Quick Pickled Jalapeños
- 2 tbsp white wine vinegar
- ½ tsp granulated sugar
- Salt and pepper to taste
- 1 tbsp ricotta cheese
- ¾ lb ground chicken
- ¼ tsp smoked paprika
- 1 tsp garlic powder
- 1 cup bread crumbs
- ¼ tsp salt

Directions:

1. Combine the jalapeños, white wine vinegar, sugar, black pepper, and salt in a bowl. Let sit the jalapeño mixture in the fridge for 15 minutes. In a bowl, combine ricotta cheese, cheddar cheese, and 1 tsp of the jalapeños. Form mixture into 8 balls. Mix the ground chicken, smoked paprika, garlic powder, and salt in a bowl. Form mixture into 8 meatballs. Form a hole in the chicken meatballs, press a cheese ball into the hole and form chicken around the cheese ball, sealing the cheese ball in meatballs.
2. Preheat air fryer at 350ºF. Mix the breadcrumbs and salt in a bowl. Roll stuffed meatballs in the mixture. Place the meatballs in the greased frying basket. Air Fry for 10 minutes, turning once. Serve immediately.

Buttermilk-fried Drumsticks

Servings: 2 | Cooking Time: 25 Minutes

Ingredients:

- 1 egg
- ½ cup buttermilk
- ¾ cup self-rising flour
- ¾ cup seasoned panko breadcrumbs
- 1 teaspoon salt
- ¼ teaspoon ground black pepper (to mix into coating)
- 4 chicken drumsticks, skin on
- oil for misting or cooking spray

Directions:

1. Beat together egg and buttermilk in shallow dish.
2. In a second shallow dish, combine the flour, panko crumbs, salt, and pepper.
3. Sprinkle chicken legs with additional salt and pepper to taste.
4. Dip legs in buttermilk mixture, then roll in panko mixture, pressing in crumbs to make coating stick. Mist with oil or cooking spray.
5. Spray air fryer basket with cooking spray.
6. Cook drumsticks at 360°F for 10minutes. Turn pieces over and cook an additional 10minutes.
7. Turn pieces to check for browning. If you have any white spots that haven't begun to brown, spritz them with oil or cooking spray. Continue cooking for 5 more minutes or until crust is golden brown and juices run clear. Larger, meatier drumsticks will take longer to cook than small ones.

Indian Chicken Tandoori

Servings: 2 | Cooking Time: 35 Minutes

Ingredients:

- 2 chicken breasts, cubed
- ½ cup hung curd
- 1 tsp turmeric powder
- 1 tsp red chili powder
- 1 tsp chaat masala powder
- Pinch of salt

Directions:

1. Preheat air fryer to 350°F. Mix the hung curd, turmeric, red chili powder, chaat masala powder, and salt in a mixing bowl. Stir until the mixture is free of lumps. Coat the chicken with the mixture, cover, and refrigerate for 30 minutes to marinate. Place the marinated chicken chunks in a baking pan and drizzle with the remaining marinade. Bake for 25 minutes until the chicken is juicy and spiced. Serve warm.

Lemon Herb Whole Cornish Hen

Servings: 2 | Cooking Time: 50 Minutes

Ingredients:

- 1 Cornish hen
- ¼ cup olive oil
- 2 tbsp lemon juice
- 2 tbsp sage, chopped
- 2 tbsp thyme, chopped
- 4 garlic cloves, chopped
- Salt and pepper to taste
- 1 celery stalk, chopped
- ½ small onion
- ½ lemon, juiced and zested
- 2 tbsp chopped parsley

Directions:

1. Preheat air fryer to 380°F. Whisk the olive oil, lemon juice, sage, thyme, garlic, salt, and pepper in a bowl. Rub the mixture on the tops and sides of the hen. Pour any excess inside the cavity of the bird. Stuff the celery, onion, and lemon juice and zest into the cavity of the hen. Put in the frying basket and Roast for 40-45 minutes. Cut the hen in half and serve garnished with parsley.

Cajun Fried Chicken

Servings: 3 | Cooking Time: 35 Minutes

Ingredients:

- 1 cup Cajun seasoning
- ½ tsp mango powder
- 6 chicken legs, bone-in

Directions:

1. Preheat air fryer to 360°F. Place half of the Cajun seasoning and 3/4 cup of water in a bowl and mix well to dissolve any lumps. Add the remaining Cajun seasoning and mango powder to a shallow bowl and stir to combine. Dip the chicken in the batter, then coat it in the mango seasoning. Lightly spritz the chicken with cooking spray. Place the chicken in the air fryer and Air Fry for 14-16 minutes, turning once until the chicken is cooked and the coating is brown. Serve and enjoy!

Sticky Drumsticks

Servings: 4 | Cooking Time: 45 Minutes

Ingredients:

- 1 lb chicken drumsticks
- 1 tbsp chicken seasoning
- 1 tsp dried chili flakes
- Salt and pepper to taste
- ¼ cup honey
- 1 cup barbecue sauce

Directions:

1. Preheat air fryer to 390°F. Season drumsticks with chicken seasoning, chili flakes, salt, and pepper. Place one batch of drumsticks in the greased frying basket and Air Fry for 18-20 minutes, flipping once until golden.
2. While the chicken is cooking, combine honey and barbecue sauce in a small bowl. Remove the drumsticks to a serving dish. Drizzle honey-barbecue sauce over and serve.

Basic Chicken Breasts

Servings:4 | Cooking Time: 15 Minutes

Ingredients:

- 2 tsp olive oil
- 2 chicken breasts
- Salt and pepper to taste
- ½ tsp garlic powder
- ½ tsp rosemary

Directions:

1. Preheat air fryer to 350ºF. Rub the chicken breasts with olive oil over tops and bottom and sprinkle with garlic powder, rosemary, salt, and pepper. Place the chicken in the frying basket and Air Fry for 9 minutes, flipping once. Let rest onto a serving plate for 5 minutes before cutting into cubes. Serve and enjoy!

Sage & Paprika Turkey Cutlets

Servings: 4 | Cooking Time: 15 Minutes

Ingredients:

- ½ cup bread crumbs
- ¼ tsp paprika
- Salt and pepper to taste
- ⅛ tsp dried sage
- ⅛ tsp garlic powder
- ¼ tsp ground cumin
- 1 egg

- 4 turkey breast cutlets
- 2 tbsp chopped chervil

Directions:

1. Preheat air fryer to 380°F. Combine the bread crumbs, paprika, salt, black pepper, sage, cumin, and garlic powder in a bowl and mix well. Beat the egg in another bowl until frothy. Dip the turkey cutlets into the egg mixture, then coat them in the bread crumb mixture. Put the breaded turkey cutlets in the frying basket. Bake for 4 minutes. Turn the cutlets over, then Bake for 4 more minutes. Decorate with chervil and serve.

Jerk Chicken Drumsticks

Servings: 2 | Cooking Time: 20 Minutes

Ingredients:

- 1 or 2 cloves garlic
- 1 inch of fresh ginger
- 2 serrano peppers, (with seeds if you like it spicy, seeds removed for less heat)
- 1 teaspoon ground allspice
- 1 teaspoon ground nutmeg
- 1 teaspoon chili powder
- ½ teaspoon dried thyme
- ½ teaspoon ground cinnamon
- ½ teaspoon paprika
- 1 tablespoon brown sugar
- 1 teaspoon soy sauce
- 2 tablespoons vegetable oil
- 6 skinless chicken drumsticks

Directions:

1. Combine all the ingredients except the chicken in a small chopper or blender and blend to a paste. Make slashes into the meat of the chicken drumsticks and rub the spice blend all over the chicken (a pair of plastic gloves makes this really easy). Transfer the rubbed chicken to a non-reactive covered container and let the chicken marinate for at least 30 minutes or overnight in the refrigerator.
2. Preheat the air fryer to 400°F.
3. Transfer the drumsticks to the air fryer basket. Air-fry for 10 minutes. Turn the drumsticks over and air-fry for another 10 minutes. Serve warm with some rice and vegetables or a green salad.

Moroccan-style Chicken Strips

Servings: 4 | Cooking Time: 30 Minutes

Ingredients:

- 4 chicken breasts, cut into strips
- 2 tsp olive oil
- 2 tbsp cornstarch
- 3 garlic cloves, minced
- ½ cup chicken broth
- ¼ cup lemon juice
- 1 tbsp honey
- ½ tsp ras el hanout
- 1 cup cooked couscous

Directions:

1. Preheat air fryer to 400°F. Mix the chicken and olive oil in a bowl, then add the cornstarch. Stir to coat. Add the garlic and transfer to a baking pan. Put the pan in the fryer. Bake for 10 minutes. Stir at least once during cooking.
2. When done, pour in the chicken broth, lemon juice, honey, and ras el hanout. Bake for an additional 6-9 minutes or until the sauce is thick and the chicken cooked through with no pink showing. Serve with couscous.

Italian Roasted Chicken Thighs

Servings: 6 | Cooking Time: 14 Minutes

Ingredients:

- 6 boneless chicken thighs
- ½ teaspoon dried oregano
- ½ teaspoon garlic powder
- ½ teaspoon sea salt
- ½ teaspoon black pepper
- ¼ teaspoon crushed red pepper flakes

Directions:

1. Pat the chicken thighs with paper towel.
2. In a small bowl, mix the oregano, garlic powder, salt, pepper, and crushed red pepper flakes. Rub the spice mixture onto the chicken thighs.
3. Preheat the air fryer to 400°F.
4. Place the chicken thighs in the air fryer basket and spray with cooking spray. Cook for 10 minutes, turn over, and cook another 4 minutes. When cooking completes, the internal temperature should read 165°F.

Mexican Chicken Roll-ups

Servings: 4 | Cooking Time: 35 Minutes

Ingredients:

- ½ red bell pepper, cut into strips
- ½ green bell pepper, cut into strips
- 2 chicken breasts
- ½ lime, juiced
- 2 tbsp taco seasoning
- 1 spring onion, thinly sliced

Directions:

1. Preheat air fryer to 400°F. Cut the chicken into cutlets by slicing the chicken breast in half horizontally in order to have 4 thin cutlets. Drizzle with lime juice and season with taco seasoning. Divide the red pepper, green pepper, and spring onion equally between the 4 cutlets. Roll up the cutlets. Secure with toothpicks. Place the chicken roll-ups in the air fryer and lightly spray with cooking oil. Bake for 12 minutes, turning once. Serve warm.

Cajun Chicken Livers

Servings: 2 | Cooking Time: 45 Minutes

Ingredients:

- 1 lb chicken livers, rinsed, connective tissue discarded
- 1 cup whole milk
- ½ cup cornmeal
- 3/4 cup flour
- 1 tsp salt and black pepper
- 1 tsp Cajun seasoning
- 2 eggs
- 1 ½ cups bread crumbs
- 1 tbsp olive oil
- 2 tbsp chopped parsley

Directions:

1. Pat chicken livers dry with paper towels, then transfer them to a small bowl and pour in the milk and black pepper. Let sit covered in the fridge for 2 hours.
2. Preheat air fryer at 375ºF. In a bowl, combine cornmeal, flour, salt, and Cajun seasoning. In another bowl, beat the eggs, and in a third bowl, add bread crumbs. Dip chicken livers first in the cornmeal mixture, then in the egg, and finally in the bread crumbs. Place chicken livers in the greased frying basket, brush the tops lightly with olive oil, and Air Fry for 16 minutes, turning once. Serve right away sprinkled with parsley.

Peachy Chicken Chunks With Cherries

Servings: 4 | Cooking Time: 16 Minutes

Ingredients:

- ⅓ cup peach preserves
- 1 teaspoon ground rosemary
- ½ teaspoon black pepper
- ½ teaspoon salt
- ½ teaspoon marjoram
- 1 teaspoon light olive oil
- 1 pound boneless chicken breasts, cut in 1½-inch chunks
- oil for misting or cooking spray
- 10-ounce package frozen unsweetened dark cherries, thawed and drained

Directions:

1. In a medium bowl, mix together peach preserves, rosemary, pepper, salt, marjoram, and olive oil.
2. Stir in chicken chunks and toss to coat well with the preserve mixture.
3. Spray air fryer basket with oil or cooking spray and lay chicken chunks in basket.
4. Cook at 390°F for 7minutes. Stir. Cook for 8 more minutes or until chicken juices run clear.
5. When chicken has cooked through, scatter the cherries over and cook for additional minute to heat cherries.

Irresistible Cheesy Chicken Sticks

Servings: 2 | Cooking Time: 30 Minutes

Ingredients:

- 6 mozzarella sticks
- 1 cup flour
- 2 eggs, beaten
- 1 lb ground chicken
- 1 ½ cups breadcrumbs
- ¼ tsp crushed chilis
- ¼ tsp cayenne pepper
- ½ tsp garlic powder
- ¼ tsp shallot powder
- ½ tsp oregano

Directions:

1. Preheat air fryer to 390°F. Combine crushed chilis, cayenne pepper, garlic powder, shallot powder, and oregano in a bowl. Add the ground chicken and mix well with your hands until evenly combined. In another mixing bowl, beat the eggs until fluffy and until the

yolks and whites are fully combined, and set aside.
2. Pour the beaten eggs, flour, and bread crumbs into 3 separate bowls. Roll the mozzarella sticks in the flour, then dip them in the beaten eggs. With hands, wrap the stick in a thin layer of the chicken mixture. Finally, coat the sticks in the crumbs. Place the sticks in the greased frying basket fryer and Air Fry for 18-20 minutes, turning once until crispy. Serve hot.

Poblano Bake

Servings: 4 | Cooking Time: 11 Minutes Per Batch

Ingredients:

- 2 large poblano peppers (approx. 5½ inches long excluding stem)
- ¾ pound ground turkey, raw
- ¾ cup cooked brown rice
- 1 teaspoon chile powder
- ½ teaspoon ground cumin
- ½ teaspoon garlic powder
- 4 ounces sharp Cheddar cheese, grated
- 1 8-ounce jar salsa, warmed

Directions:

1. Slice each pepper in half lengthwise so that you have four wide, flat pepper halves.
2. Remove seeds and membrane and discard. Rinse inside and out.
3. In a large bowl, combine turkey, rice, chile powder, cumin, and garlic powder. Mix well.
4. Divide turkey filling into 4 portions and stuff one into each of the 4 pepper halves. Press lightly to pack down.
5. Place 2 pepper halves in air fryer basket and cook at 390°F for 10minutes or until turkey is well done.
6. Top each pepper half with ¼ of the grated cheese. Cook 1 more minute or just until cheese melts.
7. Repeat steps 5 and 6 to cook remaining pepper halves.
8. To serve, place each pepper half on a plate and top with ¼ cup warm salsa.

Honey-glazed Cornish Hen

Servings:2 | Cooking Time: 40 Minutes

Ingredients:

- 2 tbsp butter, melted
- 2 tbsp Dijon mustard
- Salt and pepper to taste
- ⅛ tsp ground nutmeg
- ½ tsp honey
- 1 tbsp olive oil
- 1 Cornish game hen
- 1 tangerine, quartered

Directions:

1. Preheat air fryer to 350°F. Whisk the butter, mustard, salt, black pepper, nutmeg, and honey in a bowl. Brush olive oil over and inside of cornish hen and scatter with the honey mixture. Stuff tangerine into the hen´s cavity.
2. Place hen in the frying basket and Air Fry for 28-32 minutes, flipping twice. Transfer it to a cutting board and let rest for 5 minutes until easy to handle. Split in half by cutting down the spine and serve right away.

Gingery Turkey Meatballs

Servings: 4 | Cooking Time: 25 Minutes

Ingredients:

- ¼ cup water chestnuts, chopped
- ¼ cup panko bread crumbs
- 1 lb ground turkey
- ½ tsp ground ginger
- 2 tbsp fish sauce
- 1 tbsp sesame oil
- 1 small onion, minced
- 1 egg, beaten

Directions:

1. Preheat air fryer to 400°F. Place the ground turkey, water chestnuts, ground ginger, fish sauce, onion, egg, and bread crumbs in a bowl and stir to combine. Form the turkey mixture into 1-inch meatballs. Arrange the meatballs in the baking pan. Drizzle with sesame oil. Bake until the meatballs are cooked through, 10-12 minutes, flipping once. Serve and enjoy!

Lemon Sage Roast Chicken

Servings: 4 | Cooking Time: 60 Minutes

Ingredients:

- 1 (4-pound) chicken
- 1 bunch sage, divided
- 1 lemon, zest and juice
- salt and freshly ground black pepper

Directions:

1. Preheat the air fryer to 350°F and pour a little water into the bottom of the air fryer drawer. (This will help prevent the grease that drips into the bottom drawer from burning and smoking.)

2. Run your fingers between the skin and flesh of the chicken breasts and thighs. Push a couple of sage leaves up underneath the skin of the chicken on each breast and each thigh.
3. Push some of the lemon zest up under the skin of the chicken next to the sage. Sprinkle some of the zest inside the chicken cavity, and reserve any leftover zest. Squeeze the lemon juice all over the chicken and in the cavity as well.
4. Season the chicken, inside and out, with the salt and freshly ground black pepper. Set a few sage leaves aside for the final garnish. Crumple up the remaining sage leaves and push them into the cavity of the chicken, along with one of the squeezed lemon halves.
5. Place the chicken breast side up into the air fryer basket and air-fry for 20 minutes at 350°F. Flip the chicken over so that it is breast side down and continue to air-fry for another 20 minutes. Return the chicken to breast side up and finish air-frying for 20 more minutes. The internal temperature of the chicken should register 165°F in the thickest part of the thigh when fully cooked. Remove the chicken from the air fryer and let it rest on a cutting board for at least 5 minutes.
6. Cut the rested chicken into pieces, sprinkle with the reserved lemon zest and garnish with the reserved sage leaves.

Tortilla Crusted Chicken Breast

Servings: 2 | Cooking Time: 12 Minutes

Ingredients:

- ⅓ cup flour
- 1 teaspoon salt
- 1½ teaspoons chili powder
- 1 teaspoon ground cumin
- freshly ground black pepper
- 1 egg, beaten
- ¾ cup coarsely crushed yellow corn tortilla chips
- 2 (3- to 4-ounce) boneless chicken breasts
- vegetable oil
- ½ cup salsa
- ½ cup crumbled queso fresco
- fresh cilantro leaves
- sour cream or guacamole (optional)

Directions:

1. Set up a dredging station with three shallow dishes. Combine the flour, salt, chili powder, cumin and black pepper in the first shallow dish. Beat the egg in the second shallow dish. Place the crushed tortilla chips in the third shallow dish.
2. Dredge the chicken in the spiced flour, covering all sides of the breast. Then dip the chicken into the egg, coating the chicken completely. Finally, place the chicken into the tortilla chips and press the chips onto the chicken to make sure they adhere to all sides of the breast. Spray the coated chicken breasts on both sides with vegetable oil.
3. Preheat the air fryer to 380°F.
4. Air-fry the chicken for 6 minutes. Then turn the chicken breasts over and air-fry for another 6 minutes. (Increase the cooking time if you are using chicken breasts larger than 3 to 4 ounces.)
5. When the chicken has finished cooking, serve each breast with a little salsa, the crumbled queso fresco and cilantro as the finishing touch. Serve some sour cream and/or guacamole at the table, if desired.

Spinach And Feta Stuffed Chicken Breasts

Servings: 4 | Cooking Time: 27 Minutes

Ingredients:

- 1 (10-ounce) package frozen spinach, thawed and drained well
- 1 cup feta cheese, crumbled
- ½ teaspoon freshly ground black pepper
- 4 boneless chicken breasts
- salt and freshly ground black pepper
- 1 tablespoon olive oil

Directions:

1. Prepare the filling. Squeeze out as much liquid as possible from the thawed spinach. Rough chop the spinach and transfer it to a mixing bowl with the feta cheese and the freshly ground black pepper.
2. Prepare the chicken breast. Place the chicken breast on a cutting board and press down on the chicken breast with one hand to keep it stabilized. Make an incision about 1-inch long in the fattest side of the breast. Move the knife up and down inside the chicken breast, without poking through either the top or the bottom, or the other side of the breast. The inside pocket should be about 3-inches long, but the opening should only be about 1-inch wide. If this is too difficult, you can make the incision longer, but you will have to be more careful when cooking the chicken breast since this will expose more of the stuffing.
3. Once you have prepared the chicken breasts,

use your fingers to stuff the filling into each pocket, spreading the mixture down as far as you can.
4. Preheat the air fryer to 380°F.
5. Lightly brush or spray the air fryer basket and the chicken breasts with olive oil. Transfer two of the stuffed chicken breasts to the air fryer. Air-fry for 12 minutes, turning the chicken breasts over halfway through the cooking time. Remove the chicken to a resting plate and air-fry the second two breasts for 12 minutes. Return the first batch of chicken to the air fryer with the second batch and air-fry for 3 more minutes. When the chicken is cooked, an instant read thermometer should register 165°F in the thickest part of the chicken, as well as in the stuffing.
6. Remove the chicken breasts and let them rest on a cutting board for 2 to 3 minutes. Slice the chicken on the bias and serve with the slices fanned out.

Basic Chicken Breasts

Servings: 4 | Cooking Time: 15 Minutes

Ingredients:

- 2 tsp olive oil
- 4 chicken breasts
- Salt and pepper to taste
- 1 tbsp Italian seasoning

Directions:

1. Preheat air fryer at 350°F. Rub olive oil over chicken breasts and sprinkle with salt, Italian seasoning and black pepper. Place them in the frying basket and Air Fry for 8-10 minutes. Let rest for 5 minutes before cutting. Store it covered in the fridge for up to 1 week.

Pickle Brined Fried Chicken

Servings: 4 | Cooking Time: 47 Minutes

Ingredients:

- 4 bone-in, skin-on chicken legs, cut into drumsticks and thighs (about 3½ pounds)
- pickle juice from a 24-ounce jar of kosher dill pickles
- ½ cup flour
- salt and freshly ground black pepper
- 2 eggs
- 1 cup fine breadcrumbs
- 1 teaspoon salt
- 1 teaspoon freshly ground black pepper
- ½ teaspoon ground paprika
- ⅛ teaspoon ground cayenne pepper
- vegetable or canola oil in a spray bottle

Directions:

1. Place the chicken in a shallow dish and pour the pickle juice over the top. Cover and transfer the chicken to the refrigerator to brine in the pickle juice for 3 to 8 hours.
2. When you are ready to cook, remove the chicken from the refrigerator to let it come to room temperature while you set up a dredging station. Place the flour in a shallow dish and season well with salt and freshly ground black pepper. Whisk the eggs in a second shallow dish. In a third shallow dish, combine the breadcrumbs, salt, pepper, paprika and cayenne pepper.
3. Preheat the air fryer to 370°F.
4. Remove the chicken from the pickle brine and gently dry it with a clean kitchen towel. Dredge each piece of chicken in the flour, then dip it into the egg mixture, and finally press it into the breadcrumb mixture to coat all sides of the chicken. Place the breaded chicken on a plate or baking sheet and spray each piece all over with vegetable oil.
5. Air-fry the chicken in two batches. Place two chicken thighs and two drumsticks into the air fryer basket. Air-fry for 10 minutes. Then, gently turn the chicken pieces over and air-fry for another 10 minutes. Remove the chicken pieces and let them rest on plate – do not cover. Repeat with the second batch of chicken, air-frying for 20 minutes, turning the chicken over halfway through.
6. Lower the temperature of the air fryer to 340°F. Place the first batch of chicken on top of the second batch already in the basket and air-fry for an additional 7 minutes. Serve warm and enjoy.

Turkey Tenderloin With A Lemon Touch

Servings: 4 | Cooking Time: 45 Minutes

Ingredients:

- 1 lb boneless, skinless turkey breast tenderloin
- Salt and pepper to taste
- ½ tsp garlic powder
- ½ tsp chili powder
- ½ tsp dried thyme
- 1 lemon, juiced
- 1 tbsp chopped cilantro

Directions:

1. Preheat air fryer to 350°F. Dry the turkey com-

pletely with a paper towel, then season with salt, pepper, garlic powder, chili powder, and thyme. Place the turkey in the frying basket. Squeeze the lemon juice over the turkey and bake for 10 minutes. Turn the turkey and bake for another 10 to 15 minutes. Allow to rest for 10 minutes before slicing. Serve sprinkled with cilantro and enjoy.

Za'atar Chicken Drumsticks

Servings: 4 | Cooking Time: 45 Minutes

Ingredients:

- 2 tbsp butter, melted
- 8 chicken drumsticks
- 1 ½ tbsp Za'atar seasoning
- Salt and pepper to taste
- 1 lemon, zested
- 2 tbsp parsley, chopped

Directions:

1. Preheat air fryer to 390°F. Mix the Za'atar seasoning, lemon zest, parsley, salt, and pepper in a bowl. Add the chicken drumsticks and toss to coat. Place them in the air fryer and brush them with butter. Air Fry for 18-20 minutes, flipping once until crispy. Serve and enjoy!

Party Buffalo Chicken Drumettes

Servings: 6 | Cooking Time: 30 Minutes

Ingredients:

- 16 chicken drumettes
- 1 tsp garlic powder
- 1 tbsp chicken seasoning
- Black pepper to taste
- ¼ cup Buffalo wings sauce
- 2 spring onions, sliced

Directions:

1. Preheat air fryer to 400°F. Sprinkle garlic, chicken seasoning, and black pepper on the drumettes. Place them in the fryer and spray with cooking oil. Air Fry for 10 minutes, shaking the basket once. Transfer the drumettes to a large bowl. Drizzle with Buffalo wing sauce and toss to coat. Place in the fryer and Fry for 7-8 minutes, until crispy. Allow to cool slightly. Top with spring onions and serve warm.

Italian-inspired Chicken Pizzadillas

Servings: 4 | Cooking Time: 25 Minutes

Ingredients:

- 2 cups cooked boneless, skinless chicken, shredded
- 1 cup grated provolone cheese
- 8 basil and menta leaves, julienned
- ½ tsp salt
- 1 tsp garlic powder
- 3 tbsp butter, melted
- 8 flour tortillas
- 1 cup marinara sauce
- 1 cup grated cheddar cheese

Directions:

1. Preheat air fryer at 350ºF. Sprinkle chicken with salt and garlic powder. Brush on one side of a tortilla lightly with melted butter. Spread ¼ cup of marinara sauce, then top with ½ cup of chicken, ¼ cup of cheddar cheese, ¼ cup of provolone, and finally, ¼ of basil and menta leaves. Top with a second tortilla and lightly brush with butter on top. Repeat with the remaining ingredients. Place quesadillas, butter side down, in the frying basket and Bake for 3 minutes. Cut them into 6 sections and serve.

Simple Salsa Chicken Thighs

Servings:2 | Cooking Time: 35 Minutes

Ingredients:

- 1 lb boneless, skinless chicken thighs
- 1 cup mild chunky salsa
- ½ tsp taco seasoning
- 2 lime wedges for serving

Directions:

1. Preheat air fryer to 350ºF. Add chicken thighs into a baking pan and pour salsa and taco seasoning over. Place the pan in the frying basket and Air Fry for 30 minutes until golden brown. Serve with lime wedges.

Farmer´s Fried Chicken

Servings: 4 | Cooking Time: 55 Minutes

Ingredients:

- 3 lb whole chicken, cut into breasts, drumsticks, and thighs
- 2 cups flour
- 4 tsp salt
- 4 tsp dried basil
- 4 tsp dried thyme
- 2 tsp dried shallot powder
- 2 tsp smoked paprika
- 1 tsp mustard powder
- 1 tsp celery salt
- 1 cup kefir
- ¼ cup honey

Directions:

1. Preheat the air fryer to 370°F. Combine the flour, salt, basil, thyme, shallot, paprika, mustard powder, and celery salt in a bowl. Pour into a glass jar. Mix the kefir and honey in a large bowl and add the chicken, stir to coat. Marinate for 15 minutes at room temperature. Remove the chicken from the kefir mixture; discard the rest. Put 2/3 cup of the flour mix onto a plate and dip the chicken. Shake gently and put on a wire rack for 10 minutes. Line the frying basket with round parchment paper with holes punched in it. Place the chicken in a single layer and spray with cooking oil. Air Fry for 18-25 minutes, flipping once around minute 10. Serve hot.

Cal-mex Turkey Patties

Servings: 4 | Cooking Time: 30 Minutes

Ingredients:

- 1/3 cup crushed corn tortilla chips
- 1/3 cup grated American cheese
- 1 egg, beaten
- ¼ cup salsa
- Salt and pepper to taste
- 1 lb ground turkey
- 1 tbsp olive oil
- 1 tsp chili powder

Directions:

1. Preheat air fryer to 330°F. Mix together egg, tortilla chips, salsa, cheese, salt, and pepper in a bowl. Using your hands, add the ground turkey and mix gently until just combined. Divide the meat into 4 equal portions and shape into patties about ½ inch thick. Brush the patties with olive oil and sprinkle with chili powder. Air Fry the patties for 14-16 minutes, flipping once until cooked through and golden. Serve and enjoy!

Fish And Seafood Recipes

Catalan-style Crab Samfaina

Servings: 4 | Cooking Time: 30 Minutes

Ingredients:

- 1 peeled eggplant, cubed
- 1 zucchini, cubed
- 1 onion, chopped
- 1 red bell pepper, chopped
- 2 large tomatoes, chopped
- 1 tbsp olive oil
- ½ tsp dried thyme
- ½ tsp dried basil
- Salt and pepper to taste
- 1 ½ cups cooked crab meat

Directions:

1. Preheat air fryer to 400°F. In a pan, mix together all ingredients, except the crabmeat. Place the pan in the air fryer and Bake for 9 minutes. Remove the bowl and stir in the crabmeat. Return to the air fryer and roast for another 2-5 minutes until the vegetables are tender and ratatouille bubbling. Serve hot.

Blackened Catfish

Servings: 4 | Cooking Time: 8 Minutes

Ingredients:

- 1 teaspoon paprika
- 1 teaspoon garlic powder
- 1 teaspoon onion powder
- 1 teaspoon ground dried thyme
- ½ teaspoon ground black pepper
- ⅛ teaspoon cayenne pepper
- ½ teaspoon dried oregano
- ⅛ teaspoon crushed red pepper flakes
- 1 pound catfish filets
- ½ teaspoon sea salt
- 2 tablespoons butter, melted
- 1 tablespoon extra-virgin olive oil
- 2 tablespoons chopped parsley
- 1 lemon, cut into wedges

Directions:

1. In a small bowl, stir together the paprika, garlic powder, onion powder, thyme, black pepper, cayenne pepper, oregano, and crushed red pepper flakes.
2. Pat the fish dry with paper towels. Season the filets with sea salt and then coat with the blackening seasoning.
3. In a small bowl, mix together the butter and olive oil and drizzle over the fish filets, flipping them to coat them fully.
4. Preheat the air fryer to 350°F.
5. Place the fish in the air fryer basket and cook for 8 minutes, checking the fish for doneness after 4 minutes. The fish will flake easily when cooked.
6. Remove the fish from the air fryer. Top with chopped parsley and serve with lemon wedges.

Speedy Shrimp Paella

Servings: 4 | Cooking Time: 20 Minutes

Ingredients:

- 2 cups cooked rice
- 1 red bell pepper, chopped
- ¼ cup vegetable broth
- ½ tsp turmeric
- ½ tsp dried thyme
- 1 cup cooked small shrimp
- ½ cup baby peas
- 1 tomato, diced

Directions:

1. Preheat air fryer to 340°F. Gently combine rice, red bell pepper, broth, turmeric, and thyme in a baking pan. Bake in the air fryer until the rice is hot, about 9 minutes. Remove the pan from the air fryer and gently stir in shrimp, peas, and tomato. Return to the air fryer and cook until bubbling and all ingredients are hot, 5-8 minutes. Serve and enjoy!

Old Bay Fish `n´ Chips

Servings: 4 | Cooking Time: 40 Minutes

Ingredients:

- 2 russet potatoes, peeled
- 2 tbsp olive oil
- 4 tilapia filets
- ¼ cup flour
- Salt and pepper to taste
- 1 tsp Old Bay seasoning
- 1 lemon, zested
- 1 egg, beaten
- 1 cup panko bread crumbs

- 3 tbsp tartar sauce

Directions:

1. Preheat the air fryer to 400°F. Slice the potatoes into ½-inch-thick chips and drizzle with olive oil. Sprinkle with salt. Add the fries to the frying basket and Air Fry for 12-16 minutes, shaking once. Remove the potatoes to a plate. Cover loosely with foil to keep warm. Sprinkle the fish with salt and season with black pepper, lemon zest, and Old Bay seasoning, then lay on a plate. Put the egg in a shallow bowl and spread the panko on a separate plate. Dip the fish in the flour, then the egg, then the panko. Press to coat completely. Add half the fish to the frying basket and spray with cooking oil. Set a raised rack on the frying basket, top with the other half of the fish, and spray with cooking oil. Air Fry for 8-10 minutes until the fish flakes. Serve the fish and chips with tartar sauce.

Mexican-style Salmon Stir-fry

Servings: 4 | Cooking Time: 30 Minutes

Ingredients:

- 12 oz salmon fillets, cubed
- 1 red bell pepper, chopped
- 1 red onion, chopped
- 1 jalapeño pepper, minced
- ¼ cup salsa
- 2 tbsp tomato juice
- 2 tsp peanut oil
- 1 tsp chili powder
- 2 tbsp cilantro, chopped

Directions:

1. Preheat air fryer to 360°F. Mix salmon, bell pepper, onion, jalapeño, salsa, tomato juice, peanut oil, and chili powder in a bowl and put it into the air fryer. Air Fry for 12-14 minutes until the salmon is firm and the veggies are crispy and soft, stirring once. Serve topped with cilantro.

Fried Scallops

Servings:3 | Cooking Time: 6 Minutes

Ingredients:

- ½ cup All-purpose flour or tapioca flour
- 1 Large egg(s), well beaten
- 2 cups Corn flake crumbs (gluten-free, if a concern)
- Up to 2 teaspoons Cayenne
- 1 teaspoon Celery seeds
- 1 teaspoon Table salt
- 1 pound Sea scallops
- Vegetable oil spray

Directions:

1. Preheat the air fryer to 400°F.
2. Set up and fill three shallow soup plates or small pie plates on your counter: one for the flour; one for the beaten egg(s); and one for the corn flake crumbs, stirred with the cayenne, celery seeds, and salt until well combined.
3. One by one, dip a scallop in the flour, turning it every way to coat it thoroughly. Gently shake off any excess flour, then dip the scallop in the egg(s), turning it again to coat all sides. Let any excess egg slip back into the rest, then set the scallop in the corn flake mixture. Turn it several times, pressing gently to get an even coating on the scallop all around. Generously coat the scallop with vegetable oil spray, then set it aside on a cutting board. Coat the remaining scallops in the same way.
4. Set the scallops in the basket with as much air space between them as possible. They should not touch. Air-fry undisturbed for 6 minutes, or until lightly browned and firm.
5. Use kitchen tongs to gently transfer the scallops to a wire rack. Cool for only a minute or two before serving.

Seared Scallops In Beurre Blanc

Servings: 4 | Cooking Time: 15 Minutes

Ingredients:

- 1 lb sea scallops
- Salt and pepper to taste
- 2 tbsp butter, melted
- 1 lemon, zested and juiced
- 2 tbsp dry white wine

Directions:

1. Preheat the air fryer to 400°F. Sprinkle the scallops with salt and pepper, then set in a bowl. Combine the butter, lemon zest, lemon juice, and white wine in another bowl; mix well. Put the scallops in a baking pan and drizzle over them the mixture. Air Fry for 8-11 minutes, flipping over at about 5 minutes until opaque. Serve and enjoy!

Catfish Nuggets

Servings: 4 | Cooking Time: 7 Minutes Per Batch

Ingredients:

- 2 medium catfish fillets, cut in chunks (approximately 1 x 2 inch)
- salt and pepper
- 2 eggs
- 2 tablespoons skim milk
- ½ cup cornstarch
- 1 cup panko breadcrumbs, crushed
- oil for misting or cooking spray

Directions:

1. Season catfish chunks with salt and pepper to your liking.
2. Beat together eggs and milk in a small bowl.
3. Place cornstarch in a second small bowl.
4. Place breadcrumbs in a third small bowl.
5. Dip catfish chunks in cornstarch, dip in egg wash, shake off excess, then roll in breadcrumbs.
6. Spray all sides of catfish chunks with oil or cooking spray.
7. Place chunks in air fryer basket in a single layer, leaving space between for air circulation.
8. Cook at 390°F for 4minutes, turn, and cook an additional 3 minutes, until fish flakes easily and outside is crispy brown.
9. Repeat steps 7 and 8 to cook remaining catfish nuggets.

Maple Balsamic Glazed Salmon

Servings: 4 | Cooking Time: 10 Minutes

Ingredients:

- 4 (6-ounce) fillets of salmon
- salt and freshly ground black pepper
- vegetable oil
- ¼ cup pure maple syrup
- 3 tablespoons balsamic vinegar
- 1 teaspoon Dijon mustard

Directions:

1. Preheat the air fryer to 400°F.
2. Season the salmon well with salt and freshly ground black pepper. Spray or brush the bottom of the air fryer basket with vegetable oil and place the salmon fillets inside. Air-fry the salmon for 5 minutes.
3. While the salmon is air-frying, combine the maple syrup, balsamic vinegar and Dijon mustard in a small saucepan over medium heat and stir to blend well. Let the mixture simmer while the fish is cooking. It should start to thicken slightly, but keep your eye on it so it doesn't burn.
4. Brush the glaze on the salmon fillets and air-fry for an additional 5 minutes. The salmon should feel firm to the touch when finished and the glaze should be nicely browned on top. Brush a little more glaze on top before removing and serving with rice and vegetables, or a nice green salad.

Blackened Red Snapper

Servings: 4 | Cooking Time: 8 Minutes

Ingredients:

- 1½ teaspoons black pepper
- ¼ teaspoon thyme
- ¼ teaspoon garlic powder
- ⅛ teaspoon cayenne pepper
- 1 teaspoon olive oil
- 4 4-ounce red snapper fillet portions, skin on
- 4 thin slices lemon
- cooking spray

Directions:

1. Mix the spices and oil together to make a paste. Rub into both sides of the fish.
2. Spray air fryer basket with nonstick cooking spray and lay snapper steaks in basket, skin-side down.
3. Place a lemon slice on each piece of fish.
4. Cook at 390°F for 8 minutes. The fish will not flake when done, but it should be white through the center.

Sesame-crusted Tuna Steaks

Servings:3 | Cooking Time: 10-13 Minutes

Ingredients:

- ½ cup Sesame seeds, preferably a blend of white and black
- 1½ tablespoons Toasted sesame oil
- 3 6-ounce skinless tuna steaks

Directions:

1. Preheat the air fryer to 400°F.
2. Pour the sesame seeds on a dinner plate. Use ½ tablespoon of the sesame oil as a rub on both sides and the edges of a tuna steak. Set it in the sesame seeds, then turn it several times, pressing gently, to create an even coating of the seeds, including around the steak's edge. Set aside and continue coating the remaining steak(s).
3. When the machine is at temperature, set the steaks

in the basket with as much air space between them as possible. Air-fry undisturbed for 10 minutes for medium-rare (not USDA-approved), or 12 to 13 minutes for cooked through (USDA-approved).

4. Use a nonstick-safe spatula to transfer the steaks to serving plates. Serve hot.

Coconut Shrimp With Plum Sauce

Servings: 2 | Cooking Time: 30 Minutes

Ingredients:

- ½ lb raw shrimp, peeled
- 2 eggs
- ½ cup breadcrumbs
- 1 tsp red chili powder
- 2 tbsp dried coconut flakes
- Salt and pepper to taste
- ½ cup plum sauce

Directions:

1. Preheat air fryer to 350°F. Whisk the eggs with salt and pepper in a bowl. Dip in the shrimp, fully submerging. Combine the bread crumbs, coconut flakes, chili powder, salt, and pepper in another bowl until evenly blended. Coat the shrimp in the crumb mixture and place them in the foil-lined frying basket. Air Fry for 14-16 minutes. Halfway through the cooking time, shake the basket. Serve with plum sauce for dipping and enjoy!

Sardinas Fritas

Servings: 2 | Cooking Time: 15 Minutes

Ingredients:

- 2 cans boneless, skinless sardines in mustard sauce
- Salt and pepper to taste
- ½ cup bread crumbs
- 2 lemon wedges
- 1 tsp chopped parsley

Directions:

1. Preheat air fryer at 350°F. Add breadcrumbs, salt and black pepper to a bowl. Roll sardines in the breadcrumbs to coat. Place them in the greased frying basket and Air Fry for 6 minutes, flipping once. Transfer them to a serving dish. Serve topped with parsley and lemon wedges.

Corn & Shrimp Boil

Servings: 4 | Cooking Time: 40 Minutes

Ingredients:

- 8 frozen "mini" corn on the cob
- 1 tbsp smoked paprika
- 2 tsp dried thyme
- 1 tsp dried marjoram
- 1 tsp sea salt
- 1 tsp garlic powder
- 1 tsp onion powder
- 1 tsp cayenne pepper
- 1 lb baby potatoes, halved
- 1 tbsp olive oil
- 1 lb peeled shrimp, deveined
- 1 avocado, sliced

Directions:

1. Preheat the air fryer to 370°F.Combine the paprika, thyme, marjoram, salt, garlic, onion, and cayenne and mix well. Pour into a small glass jar. Add the potatoes, corn, and olive oil to the frying basket and sprinkle with 2 tsp of the spice mix and toss. Air Fry for 15 minutes, shaking the basket once until tender. Remove and set aside. Put the shrimp in the frying basket and sprinkle with 2 tsp of the spice mix. Air Fry for 5-8 minutes, shaking once until shrimp are tender and pink. Combine all the ingredients in the frying basket and sprinkle with 2 tsp of the spice mix. Toss to coat and cook for 1-2 more minutes or until hot. Serve topped with avocado.

Shrimp Al Pesto

Servings: 4 | Cooking Time: 10 Minutes

Ingredients:

- 1 lb peeled shrimp, deveined
- ¼ cup pesto sauce
- 1 lime, sliced
- 2 cups cooked farro

Directions:

1. Preheat air fryer to 360°F. Coat the shrimp with the pesto sauce in a bowl. Put the shrimp in a single layer in the frying basket. Put the lime slices over the shrimp and Roast for 5 minutes. Remove lime and discard. Serve the shrimp over a bed of farro pilaf. Enjoy!

Home-style Fish Sticks

Servings: 4 | Cooking Time: 30 Minutes

Ingredients:

- 1 lb cod fillets, cut into sticks
- 1 cup flour
- 1 egg
- ¼ cup cornmeal
- Salt and pepper to taste
- ¼ tsp smoked paprika
- 1 lemon

Directions:

1. Preheat air fryer at 350ºF. In a bowl, add ½ cup of flour. In another bowl, beat the egg and in a third bowl, combine the remaining flour, cornmeal, salt, black pepper and paprika. Roll the sticks in the flour, shake off excess flour. Then, dip them in the egg, shake off excess egg. Finally, dredge them in the cornmeal mixture. Place fish fingers in the greased frying basket and Air Fry for 10 minutes, flipping once. Serve with squeezed lemon.

Peppery Tilapia Roulade

Servings: 4 | Cooking Time: 25 Minutes

Ingredients:

- 4 jarred roasted red pepper slices
- 1 egg
- ½ cup breadcrumbs
- Salt and pepper to taste
- 4 tilapia fillets
- 2 tbsp butter, melted
- 4 lime wedges
- 1 tsp dill

Directions:

1. Preheat air fryer at 350ºF. Beat the egg and 2 tbsp of water in a bowl. In another bowl, mix the breadcrumbs, salt, and pepper. Place a red pepper slice and sprinkle with dill on each fish fillet. Tightly roll tilapia fillets from one short end to the other. Secure with toothpicks. Roll each fillet in the egg mixture, then dredge them in the breadcrumbs. Place fish rolls in the greased frying basket and drizzle the tops with melted butter. Roast for 6 minutes. Let rest in a serving dish for 5 minutes before removing the toothpicks. Serve with lime wedges. Enjoy!

Salmon Croquettes

Servings: 4 | Cooking Time: 8 Minutes

Ingredients:

- 1 tablespoon oil
- ½ cup breadcrumbs
- 1 14.75-ounce can salmon, drained and all skin and fat removed
- 1 egg, beaten
- ⅓ cup coarsely crushed saltine crackers (about 8 crackers)
- ½ teaspoon Old Bay Seasoning
- ½ teaspoon onion powder
- ½ teaspoon Worcestershire sauce

Directions:

1. Preheat air fryer to 390°F.
2. In a shallow dish, mix oil and breadcrumbs until crumbly.
3. In a large bowl, combine the salmon, egg, cracker crumbs, Old Bay, onion powder, and Worcestershire. Mix well and shape into 8 small patties about ½-inch thick.
4. Gently dip each patty into breadcrumb mixture and turn to coat well on all sides.
5. Cook at 390°F for 8minutes or until outside is crispy and browned.

Malaysian Shrimp With Sambal Mayo

Servings: 4 | Cooking Time: 30 Minutes

Ingredients:

- 24 jumbo shrimp, peeled and deveined
- 2/3 cup panko bread crumbs
- 3 tbsp mayonnaise
- 1 tbsp sambal oelek paste
- 2/3 cup shredded coconut
- 1 lime, zested
- ½ tsp ground coriander
- Salt to taste
- 2 tbsp flour
- 2 eggs

Directions:

1. Mix together mayonnaise and sambal oelek in a bowl. Set aside. In another bowl, stir together coconut, lime, coriander, panko bread crumbs, and salt. In a shallow bowl, add flour. In another shallow bowl, whisk eggs until blended. Season shrimp with salt. First, dip the shrimp into the flour, shake, and dip into the egg mix. Dip again in the coconut mix. Gently

press the coconut and panko to the shrimp. Preheat air fryer to 360°F. Put the shrimp in the greased frying basket and Air Fry for 8 minutes, flipping once until the crust is golden and the shrimp is cooked. Serve alongside the sweet chili mayo.

Rich Salmon Burgers With Broccoli Slaw

Servings: 4 | Cooking Time: 25 Minutes

Ingredients:

- 1 lb salmon fillets
- 1 egg
- ¼ cup dill, chopped
- 1 cup bread crumbs
- Salt to taste
- ½ tsp cayenne pepper
- 1 lime, zested
- 1 tsp fish sauce
- 4 buns
- 3 cups chopped broccoli
- ½ cup shredded carrots
- ¼ cup sunflower seeds
- 2 garlic cloves, minced
- 1 cup Greek yogurt

Directions:

1. Preheat air fryer to 360°F. Blitz the salmon fillets in your food processor until they are finely chopped. Remove to a large bowl and add egg, dill, bread crumbs, salt, and cayenne. Stir to combine. Form the mixture into 4 patties. Put them into the frying basket and Bake for 10 minutes, flipping once. Combine broccoli, carrots, sunflower seeds, garlic, salt, lime, fish sauce, and Greek yogurt in a bowl. Serve the salmon burgers onto buns with broccoli slaw. Enjoy!

Garlic And Dill Salmon

Servings: 2 | Cooking Time: 8 Minutes

Ingredients:

- 12 ounces salmon filets with skin
- 2 tablespoons melted butter
- 1 tablespoon extra-virgin olive oil
- 2 garlic cloves, minced
- 1 tablespoon fresh dill
- ½ teaspoon sea salt
- ½ lemon

Directions:

1. Pat the salmon dry with paper towels.
2. In a small bowl, mix together the melted butter, olive oil, garlic, and dill.
3. Sprinkle the top of the salmon with sea salt. Brush all sides of the salmon with the garlic and dill butter.
4. Preheat the air fryer to 350°F.
5. Place the salmon, skin side down, in the air fryer basket. Cook for 6 to 8 minutes, or until the fish flakes in the center.
6. Remove the salmon and plate on a serving platter. Squeeze fresh lemon over the top of the salmon. Serve immediately.

Lime Bay Scallops

Servings:4 | Cooking Time: 10 Minutes

Ingredients:

- 2 tbsp butter, melted
- 1 lime, juiced
- ¼ tsp salt
- 1 lb bay scallops
- 2 tbsp chopped cilantro

Directions:

1. Preheat air fryer to 350ºF. Combine all ingredients in a bowl, except for the cilantro. Place scallops in the frying basket and Air Fry for 5 minutes, tossing once. Serve immediately topped with cilantro.

Garlic-butter Lobster Tails

Servings:2 | Cooking Time: 20 Minutes

Ingredients:

- 2 lobster tails
- 1 tbsp butter, melted
- ½ tsp Old Bay Seasoning
- ½ tsp garlic powder
- 1 tbsp chopped parsley
- 2 lemon wedges

Directions:

1. Preheat air fryer to 400ºF. Using kitchen shears, cut down the middle of each lobster tail on the softer side. Carefully run your finger between the lobster meat and the shell to loosen the meat. Place lobster tails in the frying basket, cut sides up, and Air Fry for 4 minutes. Rub with butter, garlic powder and Old Bay seasoning and cook for 4 more minutes. Garnish with parsley and lemon wedges. Serve and enjoy!

Fish Goujons With Tartar Sauce

Servings: 4 | Cooking Time: 20 Minutes

Ingredients:

- ¼ cup flour
- Salt and pepper to taste
- ¼ tsp smoked paprika
- ¼ tsp dried oregano
- 1 tsp dried thyme
- 1 egg
- 4 haddock fillets
- 1 lemon, thinly sliced
- ½ cup tartar sauce

Directions:

1. Preheat air fryer to 400°F. Combine flour, salt, pepper, paprika, thyme, and oregano in a wide bowl. Whisk egg and 1 teaspoon water in another wide bowl. Slice each fillet into 4 strips. Dip the strips in the egg mixture. Then roll them in the flour mixture and coat completely. Arrange the fish strips on the greased frying basket. Air Fry for 4 minutes. Flip the fish and Air Fry for another 4 to 5 minutes until crisp. Serve warm with lemon slices and tartar sauce on the side and enjoy.

Asian-style Salmon Fillets

Servings: 4 | Cooking Time: 15 Minutes

Ingredients:

- 1 tbsp sesame oil
- 2 tbsp miso paste
- 2 tbsp tamari
- 2 tbsp soy sauce
- 2 tbsp dark brown sugar
- ½ tsp garlic powder
- ½ tsp ginger powder
- 4 salmon fillets
- 4 cups cooked brown rice
- 4 lemon slices

Directions:

1. Preheat air fryer at 375°F. In a bowl, combine all ingredients, except for salmon and cooked rice. Add 1/3 of the marinade to a shallow dish, submerge salmon fillets and let marinate covered in the fridge for 10 minutes. Reserve the remaining marinade. Place salmon fillets, skin side up, in the greased frying basket and Air Fry for 6-8 minutes, turning once, and brush with the reserved marinade. Divide cooked rice into serving dishes and top each with a salmon fillet. Pour the remaining marinade on top and serve with lemon slices on the side.

Filled Mushrooms With Crab & Cheese

Servings:6 | Cooking Time: 30 Minutes

Ingredients:

- 16 oz baby bella mushrooms, stems removed
- ½ cup lump crabmeat, shells discarded
- 2 oz feta cheese, crumbled
- 1 tsp prepared horseradish
- 1 tsp lemon juice
- Salt and pepper to taste
- 2 tbsp bread crumbs
- 2 tbsp butter, melted
- ¼ cup chopped dill

Directions:

1. Preheat air fryer to 350ºF. Combine the feta, crabmeat, horseradish, lemon juice, salt, and pepper in a bowl. Evenly stuff the crab mixture into mushroom caps, scatter bread crumbs over and drizzle with melted butter over the crumbs. Place the stuffed mushrooms in the frying basket. Bake for 10 minutes. Scatter with dill to serve.

Butternut Squash–wrapped Halibut Fillets

Servings:3 | Cooking Time: 11 Minutes

Ingredients:

- 15 Long spiralized peeled and seeded butternut squash strands
- 3 5- to 6-ounce skinless halibut fillets
- 3 tablespoons Butter, melted
- ¾ teaspoon Mild paprika
- ¾ teaspoon Table salt
- ¾ teaspoon Ground black pepper

Directions:

1. Preheat the air fryer to 375°F .
2. Hold 5 long butternut squash strands together and wrap them around a fillet. Set it aside and wrap any remaining fillet(s).
3. Mix the melted butter, paprika, salt, and pepper in a small bowl. Brush this mixture over the squash-wrapped fillets on all sides.
4. When the machine is at temperature, set the fillets in the basket with as much air space between them as

possible. Air-fry undisturbed for 10 minutes, or until the squash strands have browned but not burned. If the machine is at 360°F, you may need to add 1 minute to the cooking time. In any event, watch the fish carefully after the 8-minute mark.

5. Use a nonstick-safe spatula to gently transfer the fillets to a serving platter or plates. Cool for only a minute or so before serving.

Parmesan Fish Bites

Servings: 2 | Cooking Time: 30 Minutes

Ingredients:

- 1 haddock fillet, cut into bite-sized pieces
- 1 tbsp shredded cheddar
- 2 tbsp shredded Parmesan
- 2 eggs, beaten
- ½ cup breadcrumbs
- Salt and pepper to taste
- ½ cup mayoracha sauce

Directions:

1. Preheat air fryer to 350°F. Dip the strips in the beaten eggs. Place the bread crumbs, Parmesan, cheddar, salt and pepper in a bowl and mix well. Coat the fish strips in the dry mixture and place them on the foil-lined frying basket. Air Fry for 14-16 minutes. Halfway through the cooking time, shake the basket. When the cooking time is over, the fish will be cooked through and crust golden brown. Serve with mayoracha sauce (mixed mayo with sriracha) for dipping and enjoy!

Halibut With Coleslaw

Servings: 4 | Cooking Time: 30 Minutes

Ingredients:

- 1 bag coleslaw mix
- ¼ cup mayonnaise
- 1 tsp lemon zest
- 1 tbsp lemon juice
- 1 shredded carrot
- ½ cup buttermilk
- 1 tsp grated onion
- 4 halibut fillets
- Salt and pepper to taste

Directions:

1. Combine coleslaw mix, mayonnaise, carrot, buttermilk, onion, lemon zest, lemon juice, and salt in a bowl. Let chill the coleslaw covered in the fridge until ready to use. Preheat air fryer at 350°F. Sprinkle halibut with salt and pepper. Place them in the greased frying basket and Air Fry for 10 minutes until the fillets are opaque and flake easily with a fork. Serve with chilled coleslaw.

Sea Scallops

Servings: 4 | Cooking Time: 8 Minutes

Ingredients:

- 1½ pounds sea scallops
- salt and pepper
- 2 eggs
- ½ cup flour
- ½ cup plain breadcrumbs
- oil for misting or cooking spray

Directions:

1. Rinse scallops and remove the tough side muscle. Sprinkle to taste with salt and pepper.
2. Beat eggs together in a shallow dish. Place flour in a second shallow dish and breadcrumbs in a third.
3. Preheat air fryer to 390°F.
4. Dip scallops in flour, then eggs, and then roll in breadcrumbs. Mist with oil or cooking spray.
5. Place scallops in air fryer basket in a single layer, leaving some space between. You should be able to cook about a dozen at a time.
6. Cook at 390°F for 8 minutes, watching carefully so as not to overcook. Scallops are done when they turn opaque all the way through. They will feel slightly firm when pressed with tines of a fork.
7. Repeat step 6 to cook remaining scallops.

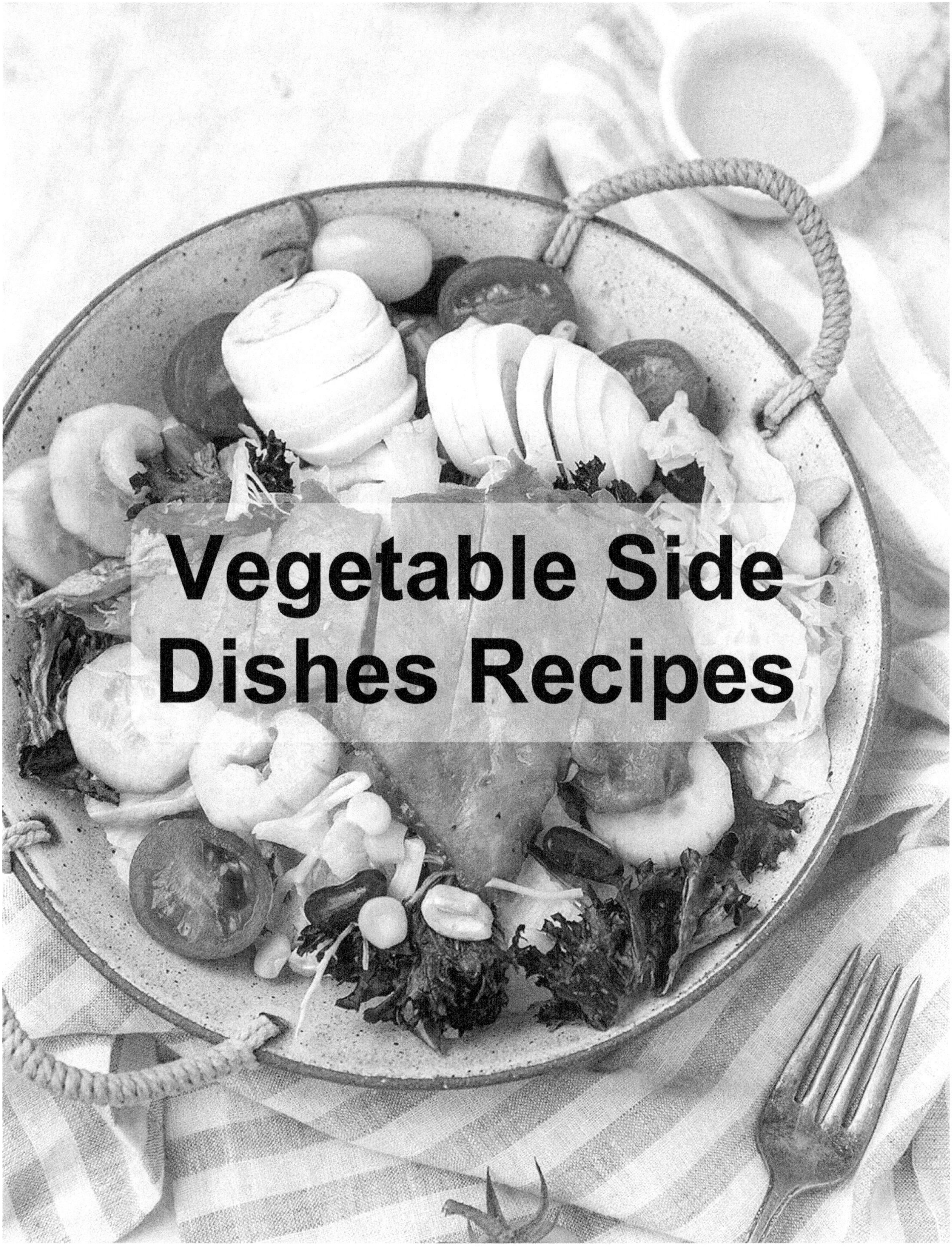

Vegetable Side Dishes Recipes

Asparagus & Cherry Tomato Roast

Servings: 6 | Cooking Time: 20 Minutes

Ingredients:

- 2 tbsp dill, chopped
- 2 cups cherry tomatoes
- 1 ½ lb asparagus, trimmed
- 2 tbsp olive oil
- 3 garlic cloves, minced
- ½ tsp salt

Directions:

1. Preheat air fryer to 380ºF. Add all ingredients to a bowl, except for dill, and toss until the vegetables are well coated with the oil. Pour the vegetable mixture into the frying basket and Roast for 11-13 minutes, shaking once. Serve topped with fresh dill.

Sweet Potato Curly Fries

Servings: 4 | Cooking Time: 10 Minutes

Ingredients:

- 2 medium sweet potatoes, washed
- 2 tablespoons avocado oil
- ¾ teaspoon salt, divided
- 1 medium avocado
- ½ teaspoon garlic powder
- ½ teaspoon paprika
- ¼ teaspoon black pepper
- ½ juice lime
- 3 tablespoons fresh cilantro

Directions:

1. Preheat the air fryer to 400°F.
2. Using a spiralizer, create curly spirals with the sweet potatoes. Keep the pieces about 1½ inches long. Continue until all the potatoes are used.
3. In a large bowl, toss the curly sweet potatoes with the avocado oil and ½ teaspoon of the salt.
4. Place the potatoes in the air fryer basket and cook for 5 minutes; shake and cook another 5 minutes.
5. While cooking, add the avocado, garlic, paprika, pepper, the remaining ¼ teaspoon of salt, lime juice, and cilantro to a blender and process until smooth. Set aside.
6. When cooking completes, remove the fries and serve warm with the lime avocado sauce.

Moroccan-spiced Carrots

Servings: 4 | Cooking Time: 30 Minutes

Ingredients:

- 1¼ pounds Baby carrots
- 2 tablespoons Butter, melted and cooled
- 1 teaspoon Mild smoked paprika
- 1 teaspoon Ground cumin
- ¾ teaspoon Ground coriander
- ¾ teaspoon Ground dried ginger
- ¼ teaspoon Ground cinnamon
- ½ teaspoon Table salt
- ¼ teaspoon Ground black pepper

Directions:

1. Preheat the air fryer to 400°F.
2. Toss the carrots, melted butter, smoked paprika, cumin, coriander, ginger, cinnamon, salt, and pepper in a large bowl until the carrots are evenly and thoroughly coated.
3. When the machine is at temperature, scrape the carrots into the basket, spreading them into as close to one layer as you can. Air-fry for 30 minutes, tossing and rearranging the carrots every 8 minutes (that is, three times), until crisp-tender and lightly browned in spots.
4. Pour the contents of the basket into a serving bowl or platter. Cool for a couple of minutes, then serve warm or at room temperature.

Fried Eggplant Slices

Servings: 3 | Cooking Time: 12 Minutes

Ingredients:

- 1½ sleeves (about 60 saltines) Saltine crackers
- ¾ cup Cornstarch
- 2 Large egg(s), well beaten
- 1 medium (about ¾ pound) Eggplant, stemmed, peeled, and cut into ¼-inch-thick rounds
- Olive oil spray

Directions:

1. Preheat the air fryer to 400°F. Also, position the rack in the center of the oven and heat the oven to 175°F.
2. Grind the saltines, in batches if necessary, in a food processor, pulsing the machine and rearranging the

saltine pieces every few pulses. Or pulverize the saltines in a large, heavy zip-closed plastic bag with the bottom of a heavy saucepan. In either case, you want small bits of saltines, not just crumbs.

3. Set up and fill three shallow soup plates or small pie plates on your counter: one for the cornstarch, one for the beaten egg(s), and one for the pulverized saltines.

4. Set an eggplant slice in the cornstarch and turn it to coat on both sides. Use a brush to lightly remove any excess. Dip it into the beaten egg(s) and turn to coat both sides. Let any excess egg slip back into the rest, then set the slice in the saltines. Turn several times, pressing gently to coat both sides evenly but not heavily. Coat both sides of the slice with olive oil spray and set it aside. Continue dipping and coating the remaining slices.

5. Set one, two, or maybe three slices in the basket. There should be at least ½ inch between them for proper air flow. Air-fry undisturbed for 12 minutes, or until crisp and browned.

6. Use a nonstick-safe spatula to transfer the slice(s) to a large baking sheet. Slip it into the oven to keep the slices warm as you air-fry more batches, as needed, always transferring the slices to the baking sheet to stay warm.

Simple Baked Potatoes With Dill Yogurt

Servings: 4 | Cooking Time: 45 Minutes

Ingredients:

- 4 Yukon gold potatoes
- Salt and black pepper
- ½ cup Greek yogurt
- ¼ cup minced dill

Directions:

1. Pierce the potatoes with a fork. Lightly coat them with sprays of cooking oil, then season with salt. Preheat air fryer to 400°F. Air Fry the potatoes in the greased frying basket for 30-35 minutes, flipping once halfway through cooking until completely cooked and slightly crispy. A knife will cut into the center of the potato with ease. Remove them to a serving dish. Add toppings of yogurt, dill, salt, and pepper to taste.

Creole Potato Wedges

Servings: 4 | Cooking Time: 10 Minutes

Ingredients:

- 1 pound medium Yukon gold potatoes
- ½ teaspoon cayenne pepper
- ½ teaspoon thyme
- ½ teaspoon garlic powder
- ½ teaspoon salt
- ½ teaspoon smoked paprika
- 1 cup dry breadcrumbs
- oil for misting or cooking spray

Directions:

1. Wash potatoes, cut into thick wedges, and drop wedges into a bowl of water to prevent browning.
2. Mix together the cayenne pepper, thyme, garlic powder, salt, paprika, and breadcrumbs and spread on a sheet of wax paper.
3. Remove potatoes from water and, without drying them, roll in the breadcrumb mixture.
4. Spray air fryer basket with oil or cooking spray and pile potato wedges into basket. It's okay if they form more than a single layer.
5. Cook at 390°F for 8minutes. Shake basket, then continue cooking for 2 minutes longer, until coating is crisp and potato centers are soft. Total cooking time will vary, depending on thickness of potato wedges.

Buttery Radish Wedges

Servings:2 | Cooking Time: 20 Minutes

Ingredients:

- 2 tbsp butter, melted
- 2 cloves garlic, minced
- ¼ tsp salt
- 20 radishes, quartered
- 2 tbsp feta cheese crumbles
- 1 tbsp chopped parsley

Directions:

1. Preheat air fryer to 370ºF. Mix the butter, garlic, and salt in a bowl. Stir in radishes. Place the radish wedges in the frying basket and Roast for 10 minutes, shaking once. Transfer to a large serving dish and stir in feta cheese. Scatter with parsley and serve.

Sweet Potato Fries

Servings: 4 | Cooking Time: 30 Minutes

Ingredients:

- 2 pounds sweet potatoes
- 1 teaspoon dried marjoram
- 2 teaspoons olive oil
- sea salt

Directions:

1. Peel and cut the potatoes into ¼-inch sticks, 4 to 5 inches long.
2. In a sealable plastic bag or bowl with lid, toss sweet potatoes with marjoram and olive oil. Rub seasonings in to coat well.
3. Pour sweet potatoes into air fryer basket and cook at 390°F for approximately 30 minutes, until cooked through with some brown spots on edges.
4. Season to taste with sea salt.

Air-fried Potato Salad

Servings: 4 | Cooking Time: 15 Minutes

Ingredients:

- 1⅓ pounds Yellow potatoes, such as Yukon Golds, cut into ½-inch chunks
- 1 large Sweet white onion(s), such as Vidalia, chopped into ½-inch pieces
- 1 tablespoon plus 2 teaspoons Olive oil
- ¾ cup Thinly sliced celery
- 6 tablespoons Regular or low-fat mayonnaise (gluten-free, if a concern)
- 2½ tablespoons Apple cider vinegar
- 1½ teaspoons Dijon mustard (gluten-free, if a concern)
- ¾ teaspoon Table salt
- ¼ teaspoon Ground black pepper

Directions:

1. Preheat the air fryer to 400°F.
2. Toss the potatoes, onion(s), and oil in a large bowl until the vegetables are glistening with oil.
3. When the machine is at temperature, transfer the vegetables to the basket, spreading them out into as even a layer as you can. Air-fry for 15 minutes, tossing and rearranging the vegetables every 3 minutes so that all surfaces get exposed to the air currents, until the vegetables are tender and even browned at the edges.
4. Pour the contents of the basket into a serving bowl. Cool for at least 5 minutes or up to 30 minutes. Add the celery, mayonnaise, vinegar, mustard, salt, and pepper. Stir well to coat. The potato salad can be made in advance; cover and refrigerate for up to 4 days.

Garlicky Bell Pepper Mix

Servings: 4 | Cooking Time: 30 Minutes

Ingredients:

- 2 tbsp vegetable oil
- ½ tsp dried cilantro
- 1 red bell pepper
- 1 yellow bell pepper
- 1 orange bell pepper
- 1 green bell pepper
- Salt and pepper to taste
- 1 head garlic

Directions:

1. Preheat air fryer to 330°F. Slice the peppers into 1-inch strips. Transfer them to a large bowl along with 1 tbsp of vegetable oil. Toss to coat. Season with cilantro, salt, and pepper. Cut the top of a garlic head and place it cut-side up on an oiled square of aluminium foil. Drizzle with vegetable oil and wrap completely in the foil.
2. Roast the wrapped garlic in the air fryer for 15 minutes. Next, add the pepper strips and roast until the peppers are tender and the garlic is soft, 6-8 minutes. Transfer the peppers to a serving dish. Remove the garlic and unwrap the foil carefully. Once cooled, squeeze the cloves out of the garlic head and mix into the peppers' dish. Serve.

Turkish Mutabal (eggplant Dip)

Servings: 2 | Cooking Time: 40 Minutes

Ingredients:

- 1 medium eggplant
- 2 tbsp tahini
- 2 tbsp lemon juice
- 1 tsp garlic powder
- ¼ tsp sumac
- 1 tsp chopped parsley

Directions:

1. Preheat air fryer to 400°F. Place the eggplant in a pan and Roast for 30 minutes, turning once. Let cool for 5-10 minutes. Scoop out the flesh and place it in a bowl. Squeeze any excess water; discard the water. Mix the flesh, tahini, lemon juice, garlic, and sumac until well combined. Scatter with parsley and serve.

Mashed Potato Tots

Servings: 18 | Cooking Time: 10 Minutes

Ingredients:

- 1 medium potato or 1 cup cooked mashed potatoes
- 1 tablespoon real bacon bits
- 2 tablespoons chopped green onions, tops only
- ¼ teaspoon onion powder
- 1 teaspoon dried chopped chives
- salt
- 2 tablespoons flour
- 1 egg white, beaten
- ½ cup panko breadcrumbs
- oil for misting or cooking spray

Directions:

1. If using cooked mashed potatoes, jump to step 4.
2. Peel potato and cut into ½-inch cubes. (Small pieces cook more quickly.) Place in saucepan, add water to cover, and heat to boil. Lower heat slightly and continue cooking just until tender, about 10minutes.
3. Drain potatoes and place in ice cold water. Allow to cool for a minute or two, then drain well and mash.
4. Preheat air fryer to 390°F.
5. In a large bowl, mix together the potatoes, bacon bits, onions, onion powder, chives, salt to taste, and flour. Add egg white and stir well.
6. Place panko crumbs on a sheet of wax paper.
7. For each tot, use about 2 teaspoons of potato mixture. To shape, drop the measure of potato mixture onto panko crumbs and push crumbs up and around potatoes to coat edges. Then turn tot over to coat other side with crumbs.
8. Mist tots with oil or cooking spray and place in air fryer basket, crowded but not stacked.
9. Cook at 390°F for 10 minutes, until browned and crispy.
10. Repeat steps 8 and 9 to cook remaining tots.

Dauphinoise (potatoes Au Gratin)

Servings: 4 | Cooking Time: 30 Minutes

Ingredients:

- ½ cup grated cheddar cheese
- 3 peeled potatoes, sliced
- ½ cup milk
- ½ cup heavy cream
- Salt and pepper to taste
- 1 tsp ground nutmeg

Directions:

1. Preheat air fryer to 350°F. Place the milk, heavy cream, salt, pepper, and nutmeg in a bowl and mix well. Dip in the potato slices and arrange on a baking dish. Spoon the remaining mixture over the potatoes. Scatter the grated cheddar cheese on top. Place the baking dish in the air fryer and Bake for 20 minutes. Serve warm and enjoy!

Classic Stuffed Shells

Servings: 4 | Cooking Time: 35 Minutes

Ingredients:

- 1 cup chopped spinach, cooked
- 1 cup shredded mozzarella
- 4 cooked jumbo shells
- 1 tsp dry oregano
- 1 cup ricotta cheese
- 1 egg, beaten
- 1 cup marinara sauce
- 1 tbsp basil leaves

Directions:

1. Preheat air fryer to 360°F. Place the beaten egg, oregano, ricotta, mozzarella, and chopped spinach in a bowl and mix until all the ingredients are combined. Fill the mixture into the cooked pasta shells. Spread half of the marinara sauce on a baking pan, then place the stuffed shells over the sauce. Spoon the remaining marinara sauce over the shells. Bake in the air fryer for 25 minutes or until the stuffed shells are wonderfully cooked, crispy on the outside with the spinach and cheeses inside gooey and delicious. Sprinkle with basil leaves and serve warm.

Perfect Asparagus

Servings: 3 | Cooking Time: 10 Minutes

Ingredients:

- 1 pound Very thin asparagus spears
- 2 tablespoons Olive oil
- 1 teaspoon Coarse sea salt or kosher salt
- ¾ teaspoon Finely grated lemon zest

Directions:

1. Preheat the air fryer to 400°F.
2. Trim just enough off the bottom of the asparagus spears so they'll fit in the basket. Put the spears on a large plate and drizzle them with some of the olive oil. Turn them over and drizzle more olive oil, working to get all the spears coated.
3. When the machine is at temperature, place the

spears in one direction in the basket. They may be touching. Air-fry for 10 minutes, tossing and rearranging the spears twice, until tender.

4. Dump the contents of the basket on a serving platter. Spread out the spears. Sprinkle them with the salt and lemon zest while still warm. Serve at once.

Zucchini Fries

Servings: 3 | Cooking Time: 12 Minutes

Ingredients:

- 1 large Zucchini
- ½ cup All-purpose flour or tapioca flour
- 2 Large egg(s), well beaten
- 1 cup Seasoned Italian-style dried bread crumbs (gluten-free, if a concern)
- Olive oil spray

Directions:

1. Preheat the air fryer to 400°F.
2. Trim the zucchini into a long rectangular block, taking off the ends and four "sides" to make this shape. Cut the block lengthwise into ½-inch-thick slices. Lay these slices flat and cut in half widthwise. Slice each of these pieces into ½-inch-thick batons.
3. Set up and fill three shallow soup plates or small pie plates on your counter: one for the flour, one for the beaten egg(s), and one for the bread crumbs.
4. Set a zucchini baton in the flour and turn it several times to coat all sides. Gently shake off any excess flour, then dip it in the egg(s), turning it to coat. Let any excess egg slip back into the rest, then set the baton in the bread crumbs and turn it several times, pressing gently to coat all sides, even the ends. Set aside on a cutting board and continue coating the remainder of the batons in the same way.
5. Lightly coat the batons on all sides with olive oil spray. Set them in two flat layers in the basket, the top layer at a 90-degree angle to the bottom one, with a little air space between the batons in each layer. In the end, the whole thing will look like a crosshatch pattern. Air-fry undisturbed for 6 minutes.
6. Use kitchen tongs to gently rearrange the batons so that any covered parts are now uncovered. The batons no longer need to be in a crosshatch pattern. Continue air-frying undisturbed for 6 minutes, or until lightly browned and crisp.
7. Gently pour the contents of the basket onto a wire rack. Spread the batons out and cool for only a minute or two before serving.

Cheese-rice Stuffed Bell Peppers

Servings: 4 | Cooking Time: 30 Minutes

Ingredients:

- 2 red bell peppers, halved and seeds and stem removed
- 1 cup cooked brown rice
- 2 tomatoes, diced
- 1 garlic clove, minced
- Salt and pepper to taste
- 4 oz goat cheese
- 3 tbsp basil, chopped
- 3 tbsp oregano, chopped
- 1 tbsp parsley, chopped
- ¼ cup grated Parmesan

Directions:

1. Preheat air fryer to 360°F. Place the brown rice, tomatoes, garlic, salt, and pepper in a bowl and stir. Divide the rice filling evenly among the bell pepper halves. Combine the goat cheese, basil, parsley and oregano in a small bowl. Sprinkle each bell pepper with the herbed cheese. Arrange the bell peppers on the air fryer and Bake for 20 minutes. Serve topped with grated Parmesan and parsley.

Sticky Broccoli Florets

Servings: 4 | Cooking Time: 20 Minutes

Ingredients:

- 4 cups broccoli florets
- 2 tbsp olive oil
- ½ tsp salt
- ½ cup grapefruit juice
- 1 tbsp raw honey
- 4-6 grapefruit wedges

Directions:

1. Preheat air fryer to 360°F. Add the broccoli, olive oil, salt, grapefruit juice, and honey to a bowl. Toss the broccoli in the liquid until well coated. Pour the broccoli mixture into the frying basket and Roast for 12 minutes, stirring once. Serve with grapefruit wedges.

Buttery Rolls

Servings: 6 | Cooking Time: 14 Minutes

Ingredients:

- 6½ tablespoons Room-temperature whole or low-fat milk
- 3 tablespoons plus 1 teaspoon Butter, melted and cooled
- 3 tablespoons plus 1 teaspoon (or 1 medium egg, well beaten) Pasteurized egg substitute, such as Egg Beaters
- 1½ tablespoons Granulated white sugar
- 1¼ teaspoons Instant yeast
- ¼ teaspoon Table salt
- 2 cups, plus more for dusting All-purpose flour
- Vegetable oil
- Additional melted butter, for brushing

Directions:

1. Stir the milk, melted butter, pasteurized egg substitute (or whole egg), sugar, yeast, and salt in a medium bowl to combine. Stir in the flour just until the mixture makes a soft dough.
2. Lightly flour a clean, dry work surface. Turn the dough out onto the work surface. Knead the dough for 5 minutes to develop the gluten.
3. Lightly oil the inside of a clean medium bowl. Gather the dough into a compact ball and set it in the bowl. Turn the dough over so that its surface has oil on it all over. Cover the bowl tightly with plastic wrap and set aside in a warm, draft-free place until the dough has doubled in bulk, about 1½ hours.
4. Punch down the dough, then turn it out onto a clean, dry work surface. Divide it into 5 even balls for a small batch, 6 balls for a medium batch, or 8 balls for a large one.
5. For a small batch, lightly oil the inside of a 6-inch round cake pan and set the balls around its perimeter, separating them as much as possible.
6. For a medium batch, lightly oil the inside of a 7-inch round cake pan and set the balls in it with one ball at its center, separating them as much as possible.
7. For a large batch, lightly oil the inside of an 8-inch round cake pan and set the balls in it with one at the center, separating them as much as possible.
8. Cover with plastic wrap and set aside to rise for 30 minutes.
9. Preheat the air fryer to 350°F .
10. Uncover the pan and brush the rolls with a little melted butter, perhaps ½ teaspoon per roll. When the machine is at temperature, set the cake pan in the basket. Air-fry undisturbed for 14 minutes, or until the rolls have risen and browned.
11. Using kitchen tongs and a nonstick-safe spatula, two hot pads, or silicone baking mitts, transfer the cake pan from the basket to a wire rack. Cool the rolls in the pan for a minute or two. Turn the rolls out onto a wire rack, set them top side up again, and cool for at least another couple of minutes before serving warm.

Grilled Lime Scallions

Servings:6 | Cooking Time: 15 Minutes

Ingredients:

- 2 bunches of scallions
- 1 tbsp olive oil
- 2 tsp lime juice
- Salt and pepper to taste
- ¼ tsp Italian seasoning
- 2 tsp lime zest

Directions:

1. Preheat air fryer to 370°F. Trim the scallions and cut them in half lengthwise. Place them in a bowl and add olive oil and lime juice. Toss to coat. Place the mix in the frying basket and Air Fry for 7 minutes, tossing once. Transfer to a serving dish and stir in salt, pepper, Italian seasoning and lime zest. Serve immediately.

Basic Corn On The Cob

Servings: 4 | Cooking Time: 15 Minutes

Ingredients:

- 3 ears of corn, shucked and halved
- 2 tbsp butter, melted
- Salt and pepper to taste
- 1 tsp minced garlic
- 1 tsp paprika

Directions:

1. Preheat air fryer at 400°F. Toss all ingredients in a bowl. Place corn in the frying basket and Bake for 7 minutes, turning once. Serve immediately.

Southern Okra Chips

Servings: 2 | Cooking Time: 20 Minutes

Ingredients:

- 2 eggs
- ¼ cup whole milk
- ¼ cup bread crumbs
- ¼ cup cornmeal
- 1 tbsp Cajun seasoning
- Salt and pepper to taste
- ⅛ tsp chili pepper
- ½ lb okra, sliced
- 1 tbsp butter, melted

Directions:

1. Preheat air fryer at 400ºF. Beat the eggs and milk in a bowl. In another bowl, combine the remaining ingredients, except okra and butter. Dip okra chips in the egg mixture, then dredge them in the breadcrumbs mixture. Place okra chips in the greased frying basket and Roast for 7 minutes, shake once and brush with melted butter. Serve right away.

Roasted Herbed Shiitake Mushrooms

Cooking Time: 5 Minutes | Servings: 4

Ingredients:

- 8 ounces shiitake mushrooms, stems removed and caps roughly chopped
- 1 tablespoon olive oil
- ½ teaspoon salt
- freshly ground black pepper
- 1 teaspoon chopped fresh thyme leaves
- 1 teaspoon chopped fresh oregano
- 1 tablespoon chopped fresh parsley

Directions:

1. Preheat the air fryer to 400°F.
2. Toss the mushrooms with the olive oil, salt, pepper, thyme and oregano. Air-fry for 5 minutes, shaking the basket once or twice during the cooking process. The mushrooms will still be somewhat chewy with a meaty texture. If you'd like them a little more tender, add a couple of minutes to this cooking time.
3. Once cooked, add the parsley to the mushrooms and toss. Season again to taste and serve.

Fried Corn On The Cob

Servings: 2 | Cooking Time: 10 Minutes

Ingredients:

- 1½ tablespoons Regular or low-fat mayonnaise (not fat-free; gluten-free, if a concern)
- 1½ teaspoons Minced garlic
- ¼ teaspoon Table salt
- ¾ cup Plain panko bread crumbs (gluten-free, if a concern)
- 3 4-inch lengths husked and de-silked corn on the cob
- Vegetable oil spray

Directions:

1. Preheat the air fryer to 400°F.
2. Stir the mayonnaise, garlic, and salt in a small bowl until well combined. Spread the panko on a dinner plate.
3. Brush the mayonnaise mixture over the kernels of a piece of corn on the cob. Set the corn in the bread crumbs, then roll, pressing gently, to coat it. Lightly coat with vegetable oil spray. Set it aside, then coat the remaining piece(s) of corn in the same way.
4. Set the coated corn on the cob in the basket with as much air space between the pieces as possible. Air-fry undisturbed for 10 minutes, or until brown and crisp along the coating.
5. Use kitchen tongs to gently transfer the pieces of corn to a wire rack. Cool for 5 minutes before serving.

Tasty Brussels Sprouts With Guanciale

Servings: 4 | Cooking Time: 50 Minutes

Ingredients:

- 3 guanciale slices, halved
- 1 lb Brussels sprouts, halved
- 2 tbsp olive oil
- ¼ tsp salt
- ¼ tsp dried thyme

Directions:

1. Preheat air fryer to 350°F. Air Fry Lay the guanciale in the air fryer, until crispy, 10 minutes. Remove and drain on a paper towel. Give the guanciale a rough chop and Set aside. Coat Brussels sprouts with olive oil in a large bowl. Add salt and thyme, then toss. Place the sprouts in the frying basket. Air Fry for about 12-15 minutes, shake the basket once until the sprouts are golden and tender. Top with guanciale and serve.

Pork Tenderloin Salad

Servings: 4 | Cooking Time: 25 Minutes

Ingredients:

- Pork Tenderloin
- ½ teaspoon smoked paprika
- ¼ teaspoon salt
- ¼ teaspoon garlic powder
- ½ teaspoon onion powder
- ⅛ teaspoon ginger
- 1 teaspoon extra-light olive oil
- ¾ pound pork tenderloin
- Dressing
- 3 tablespoons extra-light olive oil
- 2 tablespoons red wine vinegar
- 2 tablespoons Dijon mustard
- 1 tablespoon honey
- Salad
- ¼ sweet red bell pepper
- 1 large Granny Smith apple
- 8 cups shredded Napa cabbage

Directions:

1. Mix the tenderloin seasonings together with oil and rub all over surface of meat.
2. Place pork tenderloin in the air fryer basket and cook at 390°F for 25minutes, until meat registers 130°F on a meat thermometer.
3. Allow meat to rest while preparing salad and dressing.
4. In a jar, shake all dressing ingredients together until well mixed.
5. Cut the bell pepper into slivers, then core, quarter, and slice the apple crosswise.
6. In a large bowl, toss together the cabbage, bell pepper, apple, and dressing.
7. Divide salad mixture among 4 plates.
8. Slice pork tenderloin into ½-inch slices and divide among the 4 salads.
9. Serve with sweet potato or other vegetable chips.

Florentine Stuffed Tomatoes

Cooking Time: 12 Minutes | Servings: 2

Ingredients:

- 1 cup frozen spinach, thawed and squeezed dry
- ¼ cup toasted pine nuts
- ¼ cup grated mozzarella cheese
- ½ cup crumbled feta cheese
- ½ cup coarse fresh breadcrumbs
- 1 tablespoon olive oil
- salt and freshly ground black pepper
- 2 to 3 beefsteak tomatoes, halved horizontally and insides scooped out

Directions:

1. Combine the spinach, pine nuts, mozzarella and feta cheeses, breadcrumbs, olive oil, salt and freshly ground black pepper in a bowl. Spoon the mixture into the tomato halves. You should have enough filling for 2 to 3 tomatoes, depending on how big they are.
2. Preheat the air fryer to 350°F.
3. Place three or four tomato halves (depending on whether you're using 2 or 3 tomatoes and how big they are) into the air fryer and air-fry for 12 minutes. The tomatoes should be soft but still manageable and the tops should be lightly browned. Repeat with second batch if necessary.
4. Let the tomatoes cool for just a minute or two before serving.

Patatas Bravas

Servings: 4 | Cooking Time: 35 Minutes

Ingredients:

- 1 lb baby potatoes
- 1 onion, chopped
- 4 garlic cloves, minced
- 2 jalapeño peppers, minced
- 2 tsp olive oil
- 2 tsp Chile de Árbol, ground
- ½ tsp ground cumin
- ½ tsp dried oregano

Directions:

1. Preheat air fryer to 370°F. Put the baby potatoes, onion, garlic, and jalapeños in a bowl, stir, then pour in the olive oil and stir again to coat. Season with ground chile de Árbol, cumin, and oregano, and stir once again. Put the bowl in the air fryer and Air Fry for 22-28 minutes, shake the bowl once. Serve hot.

Crispy, Cheesy Leeks

Servings: 4 | Cooking Time: 15 Minutes

Ingredients:

- 2 Medium leek(s), about 9 ounces each
- Olive oil spray
- ¼ cup Seasoned Italian-style dried bread crumbs (gluten-free, if a concern)
- ¼ cup (about ¾ ounce) Finely grated Parmesan cheese
- 2 tablespoons Olive oil

Directions:

1. Preheat the air fryer to 350°F .
2. Trim off the root end of the leek(s) as well as the dark green top(s), leaving about a 5-inch usable section. Split the leek section(s) in half lengthwise. Set the leek halves cut side up on your work surface. Pull out and remove in one piece the semicircles that make up the inner structure of the leek, about halfway down. Set the removed "inside" next to the outer leek "shells" on your cutting board. Generously coat them all on all sides (particularly the "bottoms") with olive oil spray.
3. Set the leeks and their insides cut side up in the basket with as much air space between them as possible. Air-fry undisturbed for 12 minutes.
4. Meanwhile, mix the bread crumbs, cheese, and olive oil in a small bowl until well combined.
5. After 12 minutes in the air fryer, sprinkle this mixture inside the leek shells and on top of the leek insides. Increase the machine's temperature to 375°F (or 380°F or 390°F, if one of these is the closest setting). Air-fry undisturbed for 3 minutes, or until the topping is lightly browned.
6. Use a nonstick-safe spatula to transfer the leeks to a serving platter. Cool for a few minutes before serving warm.

Cauliflower

Servings: 4 | Cooking Time: 6 Minutes

Ingredients:

- ½ cup water
- 1 10-ounce package frozen cauliflower (florets)
- 1 teaspoon lemon pepper seasoning

Directions:

1. Pour the water into air fryer drawer.
2. Pour the frozen cauliflower into the air fryer basket and sprinkle with lemon pepper seasoning.
3. Cook at 390°F for approximately 6 minutes.

Vegetarians Recipes

Sweet Corn Bread

Servings: 6 | Cooking Time: 35 Minutes

Ingredients:

- 2 eggs, beaten
- ½ cup cornmeal
- ½ cup pastry flour
- 1/3 cup sugar
- 1 tsp lemon zest
- ½ tbsp baking powder
- ¼ tsp salt
- ¼ tsp baking soda
- ½ tbsp lemon juice
- ½ cup milk
- ¼ cup sunflower oil

Directions:

1. Preheat air fryer to 350°F. Add the cornmeal, flour, sugar, lemon zest, baking powder, salt, and baking soda in a bowl. Stir with a whisk until combined. Add the eggs, lemon juice, milk, and oil to another bowl and stir well. Add the wet mixture to the dry mixture and stir gently until combined. Spray a baking pan with oil. Pour the batter in and Bake in the fryer for 25 minutes or until golden and a knife inserted in the center comes out clean. Cut into wedges and serve.

Gorgeous Jalapeño Poppers

Servings: 6 | Cooking Time: 25 Minutes

Ingredients:

- 6 center-cut bacon slices, halved
- 6 jalapeños, halved lengthwise
- 4 oz cream cheese
- ¼ cup grated Gruyere cheese
- 2 tbsp chives, chopped

Directions:

1. Scoop out seeds and membranes of the jalapeño halves, discard. Combine cream cheese, Gruyere cheese, and chives in a bowl. Fill the jalapeño halves with the cream cheese filling using a small spoon. Wrap each pepper with a slice of bacon and secure with a toothpick.
2. Preheat air fryer to 325°F. Put the stuffed peppers in a single layer on the greased frying basket and Bake until the peppers are tender, cheese is melted, and the bacon is brown, 11-13minutes. Serve warm and enjoy!

Crispy Avocados With Pico De Gallo

Servings:2 | Cooking Time: 15 Minutes

Ingredients:

- 1 cup diced tomatoes
- 1 tbsp lime juice
- 1 tsp lime zest
- 2 tbsp chopped cilantro
- 1 serrano chiles, minced
- 2 cloves garlic, minced
- 1 tbsp diced white onions
- ½ tsp salt
- 2 avocados, halved and pitted
- 4 tbsp cheddar shreds

Directions:

1. Preheat air fryer to 350ºF. Combine all ingredients, except for avocados and cheddar cheese, in a bowl and let chill covered in the fridge. Place avocado halves, cut sides-up, in the frying basket, scatter cheese shreds over top of avocado halves, and Air Fry for 4 minutes. Top with pico de gallo and serve.

Sushi-style Deviled Eggs

Servings:4 | Cooking Time: 20 Minutes

Ingredients:

- ¼ cup crabmeat, shells discarded
- 4 eggs
- 2 tbsp mayonnaise
- ½ tsp soy sauce
- ¼ avocado, diced
- ¼ tsp wasabi powder
- 2 tbsp diced cucumber
- 1 sheet nori, sliced
- 8 jarred pickled ginger slices
- 1 tsp toasted sesame seeds
- 2 spring onions, sliced

Directions:

1. Preheat air fryer to 260ºF. Place the eggs in muffin cups to avoid bumping around and cracking during the cooking process. Add silicone cups to the frying basket and Air Fry for 15 minutes. Remove and plunge the eggs immediately into an ice bath to cool, about 5

minutes. Carefully peel and slice them in half lengthwise. Spoon yolks into a separate medium bowl and arrange white halves on a large plate. Mash the yolks with a fork. Stir in mayonnaise, soy sauce, avocado, and wasabi powder until smooth. Mix in cucumber and spoon into white halves. Scatter eggs with crabmeat, nori, pickled ginger, spring onions and sesame seeds to serve.

Veggie Samosas

Servings: 6 | Cooking Time: 30 Minutes

Ingredients:

- 2 tbsp cream cheese, softened
- 3 tbsp minced onion
- 2 garlic cloves, minced
- 2 tbsp grated carrots
- 3 tsp olive oil
- 3 tbsp cooked green lentils
- 6 phyllo dough sheets

Directions:

1. Preheat air fryer to 390°F. Toss the onion, garlic, carrots, and some oil in a baking pan and stir. Place in the fryer and Air Fry for 2-4 minutes until the veggies are soft. Pour into a bowl. Add the lentils and cream cheese; let chill.
2. To make the dough, first lay a sheet of phyllo on a clean workspace and spritz with some olive oil, then add a second sheet on top. Repeat with the rest of the phyllo sheets until you have 3 stacks of 2 layers. Cut the stacks into 4 lengthwise strips. Add 2 tsp of the veggie mix at the bottom of each strip, then make a triangle by lifting one corner over the filling. Continue the triangle making, like folding a flag, and seal with water. Repeat until all strips are filled and folded. Bake the samosas in the air fryer for 4-7 minutes, until golden and crisp. Serve warm.

Tomato & Squash Stuffed Mushrooms

Servings:2 | Cooking Time: 15 Minutes

Ingredients:

- 12 whole white button mushrooms
- 3 tsp olive oil
- 2 tbsp diced zucchini
- 1 tsp soy sauce
- ¼ tsp salt
- 2 tbsp tomato paste
- 1 tbsp chopped parsley

Directions:

1. Preheat air fryer to 350ºF. Remove the stems from the mushrooms. Chop the stems finely and set in a bowl. Brush 1 tsp of olive oil around the top ridge of mushroom caps. To the bowl of the stem, add all ingredients, except for parsley, and mix. Divide and press mixture into tops of mushroom caps. Place the mushrooms in the frying basket and Air Fry for 5 minutes. Top with parsley. Serve.

Bengali Samosa With Mango Chutney

Servings: 4 | Cooking Time: 65 Minutes

Ingredients:

- ¼ tsp ground fenugreek seeds
- 1 cup diced mango
- 1 tbsp minced red onion
- 2 tsp honey
- 1 tsp minced ginger
- 1 tsp apple cider vinegar
- 1 phyllo dough sheet
- 2 tbsp olive oil
- 1 potato, mashed
- ½ tsp garam masala
- ¼ tsp ground turmeric
- ⅛ tsp chili powder
- ¼ tsp ground cumin
- ½ cup green peas
- 2 scallions, chopped

Directions:

1. Mash mango in a small bowl until chunky. Stir in onion, ginger, honey, and vinegar. Save in the fridge until ready to use. Place the mashed potato in a bowl. Add half of the olive oil, garam masala, turmeric, chili powder, ground fenugreek seeds, cumin, and salt and stir until mostly smooth. Stir in peas and scallions.
2. Preheat air fryer to 425°F. Lightly flour a flat work surface and transfer the phyllo dough. Cut into 8 equal portions and roll each portion to ¼-inch thick rounds. Divide the potato filling between the dough rounds. Fold in three sides and pinch at the meeting point, almost like a pyramid. Arrange the samosas in the frying basket and brush with the remaining olive oil. Bake for 10 minutes, then flip the samosas. Bake for another 4-6 minutes until the crust is crisp and golden. Serve with mango chutney.

Two-cheese Grilled Sandwiches

Servings: 2 | Cooking Time: 30 Minutes

Ingredients:

- 4 sourdough bread slices
- 2 cheddar cheese slices
- 2 Swiss cheese slices
- 1 tbsp butter
- 2 dill pickles, sliced

Directions:

1. Preheat air fryer to 360°F. Smear both sides of the sourdough bread with butter and place them in the frying basket. Toast the bread for 6 minutes, flipping once.
2. Divide the cheddar cheese between 2 of the bread slices. Cover the remaining 2 bread slices with Swiss cheese slices. Bake for 10 more minutes until the cheeses have melted and lightly bubbled and the bread has golden brown. Set the cheddar-covered bread slices on a serving plate, cover with pickles, and top each with the Swiss-covered slices. Serve and enjoy!

Veggie Burgers

Servings: 4 | Cooking Time: 15 Minutes

Ingredients:

- 2 cans black beans, rinsed and drained
- ½ cup cooked quinoa
- ½ cup shredded raw sweet potato
- ¼ cup diced red onion
- 2 teaspoons ground cumin
- 1 teaspoon coriander powder
- ½ teaspoon salt
- oil for misting or cooking spray
- 8 slices bread
- suggested toppings: lettuce, tomato, red onion, Pepper Jack cheese, guacamole

Directions:

1. In a medium bowl, mash the beans with a fork.
2. Add the quinoa, sweet potato, onion, cumin, coriander, and salt and mix well with the fork.
3. Shape into 4 patties, each ¾-inch thick.
4. Mist both sides with oil or cooking spray and also mist the basket.
5. Cook at 390°F for 15minutes.
6. Follow the recipe for Toast, Plain & Simple.
7. Pop the veggie burgers back in the air fryer for a minute or two to reheat if necessary.
8. Serve on the toast with your favorite burger toppings.

Charred Cauliflower Tacos

Servings: 4 | Cooking Time: 10 Minutes

Ingredients:

- 1 head cauliflower, washed and cut into florets
- 2 tablespoons avocado oil
- 2 teaspoons taco seasoning
- 1 medium avocado
- ½ teaspoon garlic powder
- ¼ teaspoon black pepper
- ¼ teaspoon salt
- 2 tablespoons chopped red onion
- 2 teaspoons fresh squeezed lime juice
- ¼ cup chopped cilantro
- Eight 6-inch corn tortillas
- ½ cup cooked corn
- ½ cup shredded purple cabbage

Directions:

1. Preheat the air fryer to 390°F.
2. In a large bowl, toss the cauliflower with the avocado oil and taco seasoning. Set the metal trivet inside the air fryer basket and liberally spray with olive oil.
3. Place the cauliflower onto the trivet and cook for 10 minutes, shaking every 3 minutes to allow for an even char.
4. While the cauliflower is cooking, prepare the avocado sauce. In a medium bowl, mash the avocado; then mix in the garlic powder, pepper, salt, and onion. Stir in the lime juice and cilantro; set aside.
5. Remove the cauliflower from the air fryer basket.
6. Place 1 tablespoon of avocado sauce in the middle of a tortilla, and top with corn, cabbage, and charred cauliflower. Repeat with the remaining tortillas. Serve immediately.

Pizza Margherita With Spinach

Servings: 4 | Cooking Time: 50 Minutes

Ingredients:

- ½ cup pizza sauce
- 1 tsp dried oregano
- 1 tsp garlic powder
- 1 pizza dough
- 1 cup baby spinach
- ½ cup mozzarella cheese

Directions:

1. Preheat air fryer to 400°F. Whisk pizza sauce, oregano, and garlic in a bowl. Set aside. Form 4 balls

with the pizza dough and roll out each into a 6-inch round pizza.
2. Lay one crust in the basket, spread ¼ of the sauce, then scatter with ¼ of spinach, and finally top with mozzarella cheese. Grill for 8 minutes until golden brown and the crust is crispy. Repeat the process with the remaining crusts. Serve immediately.

Curried Potato, Cauliflower And Pea Turnovers

Servings: 4 | Cooking Time: 40 Minutes

Ingredients:

- Dough:
- 2 cups all-purpose flour
- ½ teaspoon baking powder
- 1 teaspoon salt
- freshly ground black pepper
- ¼ teaspoon dried thyme
- ¼ cup canola oil
- ½ to ⅔ cup water
- Turnover Filling:
- 1 tablespoon canola or vegetable oil
- 1 onion, finely chopped
- 1 clove garlic, minced
- 1 tablespoon grated fresh ginger
- ½ teaspoon cumin seeds
- ½ teaspoon fennel seeds
- 1 teaspoon curry powder
- 2 russet potatoes, diced
- 2 cups cauliflower florets
- ½ cup frozen peas
- 2 tablespoons chopped fresh cilantro
- salt and freshly ground black pepper
- 2 tablespoons butter, melted
- mango chutney, for serving

Directions:

1. Start by making the dough. Combine the flour, baking powder, salt, pepper and dried thyme in a mixing bowl or the bowl of a stand mixer. Drizzle in the canola oil and pinch it together with your fingers to turn the flour into a crumby mixture. Stir in the water (enough to bring the dough together). Knead the dough for 5 minutes or so until it is smooth. Add a little more water or flour as needed. Let the dough rest while you make the turnover filling.
2. Preheat a large skillet on the stovetop over medium-high heat. Add the oil and sauté the onion until it starts to become tender – about 4 minutes. Add the garlic and ginger and continue to cook for another minute. Add the dried spices and toss everything to coat. Add the potatoes and cauliflower to the skillet and pour in 1½ cups of water. Simmer everything together for 20 to 25 minutes, or until the potatoes are soft and most of the water has evaporated. If the water has evaporated and the vegetables still need more time, just add a little water and continue to simmer until everything is tender. Stir well, crushing the potatoes and cauliflower a little as you do so. Stir in the peas and cilantro, season to taste with salt and freshly ground black pepper and set aside to cool.
3. Divide the dough into 4 balls. Roll the dough balls out into ¼-inch thick circles. Divide the cooled potato filling between the dough circles, placing a mound of the filling on one side of each piece of dough, leaving an empty border around the edge of the dough. Brush the edges of the dough with a little water and fold one edge of circle over the filling to meet the other edge of the circle, creating a half moon. Pinch the edges together with your fingers and then press the edge with the tines of a fork to decorate and seal.
4. Preheat the air fryer to 380°F.
5. Spray or brush the air fryer basket with oil. Brush the turnovers with the melted butter and place 2 turnovers into the air fryer basket. Air-fry for 15 minutes. Flip the turnovers over and air-fry for another 5 minutes. Repeat with the remaining 2 turnovers.
6. These will be very hot when they come out of the air fryer. Let them cool for at least 20 minutes before serving warm with mango chutney.

Vietnamese Gingered Tofu

Servings: 4 | Cooking Time: 25 Minutes

Ingredients:

- 1 package extra-firm tofu, cubed
- 4 tsp shoyu
- 1 tsp onion powder
- ½ tsp garlic powder
- ½ tsp ginger powder
- ½ tsp turmeric powder
- Black pepper to taste
- 2 tbsp nutritional yeast
- 1 tsp dried rosemary
- 1 tsp dried dill
- 2 tsp cornstarch
- 2 tsp sunflower oil

Directions:

1. Sprinkle the tofu with shoyu and toss to coat. Add the onion, garlic, ginger, turmeric, and pepper. Gently toss to coat. Add the yeast, rosemary, dill, and cornstarch. Toss to coat. Dribble with the oil and toss again.
2. Preheat air fryer to 390°F. Spray the fryer basket with oil, put the tofu in the basket and Bake for 7 minutes. Remove, shake gently, and cook for another 7 minutes or until the tofu is crispy and golden. Serve warm.

Breaded Avocado Tacos

Servings: 3 | Cooking Time: 20 Minutes

Ingredients:

- 2 tomatoes, diced
- ¼ cup diced red onion
- 1 jalapeño, finely diced
- 1 tbsp lime juice
- 1 tsp lime zest
- ¼ cup chopped cilantro
- 1 tsp salt
- 1 egg
- 2 tbsp milk
- 1 cup crumbs
- ¼ cup of almond flour
- 1 avocado, sliced into fries
- 6 flour tortillas
- 1 cup coleslaw mix

Directions:

1. In a bowl, combine the tomatoes, jalapeño, red onion, lime juice, lime zest, cilantro, and salt. Let chill the pico de gallo covered in the fridge until ready to use.
2. Preheat air fryer at 375°F. In a small bowl, beat egg and milk. In another bowl, add breadcrumbs. Dip avocado slices in the egg mixture, then dredge them in the mixed almond flour and breadcrumbs. Place avocado slices in the greased frying basket and Air Fry for 5 minutes. Add 2 avocado fries to each tortilla. Top each with coleslaw mix. Serve immediately.

Lentil Burritos With Cilantro Chutney

Servings: 4 | Cooking Time: 30 Minutes

Ingredients:

- 1 cup cilantro chutney
- 1 lb cooked potatoes, mashed
- 2 tsp sunflower oil
- 3 garlic cloves, minced
- 1 ½ tbsp fresh lime juice
- 1 ½ tsp cumin powder
- 1 tsp onion powder
- 1 tsp coriander powder
- Salt to taste
- ½ tsp turmeric
- ¼ tsp cayenne powder
- 4 large flour tortillas
- 1 cup cooked lentils
- ½ cup shredded cabbage
- ¼ cup minced red onions

Directions:

1. Preheat air fryer to 390°F. Place the mashed potatoes, sunflower oil, garlic, lime, cumin, onion powder, coriander, salt, turmeric, and cayenne in a large bowl. Stir well until combined. Lay the tortillas out flat on the counter. In the middle of each, distribute the potato filling. Add some of the lentils, cabbage, and red onions on top of the potatoes. Close the wraps by folding the bottom of the tortillas up and over the filling, then folding the sides in, then roll the bottom up to form a burrito. Place the wraps in the greased frying basket, seam side down. Air Fry for 6-8 minutes, flipping once until golden and crispy. Serve topped with cilantro chutney.

Quinoa Burgers With Feta Cheese And Dill

Servings: 6 | Cooking Time: 10 Minutes

Ingredients:

- 1 cup quinoa (red, white or multi-colored)
- 1½ cups water
- 1 teaspoon salt
- freshly ground black pepper
- 1½ cups rolled oats
- 3 eggs, lightly beaten
- ¼ cup minced white onion
- ½ cup crumbled feta cheese
- ¼ cup chopped fresh dill
- salt and freshly ground black pepper

- vegetable or canola oil, in a spray bottle
- whole-wheat hamburger buns (or gluten-free hamburger buns*)
- arugula
- tomato, sliced
- red onion, sliced
- mayonnaise

Directions:

1. Make the quinoa: Rinse the quinoa in cold water in a saucepan, swirling it with your hand until any dry husks rise to the surface. Drain the quinoa as well as you can and then put the saucepan on the stovetop to dry and toast the quinoa. Turn the heat to medium-high and shake the pan regularly until you see the quinoa moving easily and can hear the seeds moving in the pan, indicating that they are dry. Add the water, salt and pepper. Bring the liquid to a boil and then reduce the heat to low or medium-low. You should see just a few bubbles, not a boil. Cover with a lid, leaving it askew and simmer for 20 minutes. Turn the heat off and fluff the quinoa with a fork. If there's any liquid left in the bottom of the pot, place it back on the burner for another 3 minutes or so. Spread the cooked quinoa out on a sheet pan to cool.
2. Combine the room temperature quinoa in a large bowl with the oats, eggs, onion, cheese and dill. Season with salt and pepper and mix well (remember that feta cheese is salty). Shape the mixture into 6 patties with flat sides (so they fit more easily into the air fryer). Add a little water or a few more rolled oats if necessary to get the mixture to be the right consistency to make patties.
3. Preheat the air-fryer to 400°F.
4. Spray both sides of the patties generously with oil and transfer them to the air fryer basket in one layer (you will probably have to cook these burgers in batches, depending on the size of your air fryer). Air-fry each batch at 400°F for 10 minutes, flipping the burgers over halfway through the cooking time.
5. Build your burger on the whole-wheat hamburger buns with arugula, tomato, red onion and mayonnaise.

Vegetable Couscous

Servings: 4 | Cooking Time: 10 Minutes

Ingredients:

- 4 ounces white mushrooms, sliced
- ½ medium green bell pepper, julienned
- 1 cup cubed zucchini
- ¼ small onion, slivered
- 1 stalk celery, thinly sliced
- ¼ teaspoon ground coriander
- ¼ teaspoon ground cumin
- salt and pepper
- 1 tablespoon olive oil
- Couscous
- ¾ cup uncooked couscous
- 1 cup vegetable broth or water
- ½ teaspoon salt (omit if using salted broth)

Directions:

1. Combine all vegetables in large bowl. Sprinkle with coriander, cumin, and salt and pepper to taste. Stir well, add olive oil, and stir again to coat vegetables evenly.
2. Place vegetables in air fryer basket and cook at 390°F for 5minutes. Stir and cook for 5 more minutes, until tender.
3. While vegetables are cooking, prepare the couscous: Place broth or water and salt in large saucepan. Heat to boiling, stir in couscous, cover, and remove from heat.
4. Let couscous sit for 5minutes, stir in cooked vegetables, and serve hot.

Tandoori Paneer Naan Pizza

Servings: 4 | Cooking Time: 10 Minutes

Ingredients:

- 6 tablespoons plain Greek yogurt, divided
- 1¼ teaspoons garam marsala, divided
- ½ teaspoon turmeric, divided
- ¼ teaspoon garlic powder
- ½ teaspoon paprika, divided
- ½ teaspoon black pepper, divided
- 3 ounces paneer, cut into small cubes
- 1 tablespoon extra-virgin olive oil
- 2 teaspoons minced garlic
- 4 cups baby spinach
- 2 tablespoons marinara sauce
- ¼ teaspoon salt
- 2 plain naan breads (approximately 6 inches in diameter)

- ½ cup shredded part-skim mozzarella cheese

Directions:

1. Preheat the air fryer to 350°F.
2. In a small bowl, mix 2 tablespoons of the yogurt, ½ teaspoon of the garam marsala, ¼ teaspoon of the turmeric, the garlic powder, ¼ teaspoon of the paprika, and ¼ teaspoon of the black pepper. Toss the paneer cubes in the mixture and let marinate for at least an hour.
3. Meanwhile, in a pan, heat the olive oil over medium heat. Add in the minced garlic and sauté for 1 minute. Stir in the spinach and begin to cook until it wilts. Add in the remaining 4 tablespoons of yogurt and the marinara sauce. Stir in the remaining ¾ teaspoon of garam masala, the remaining ¼ teaspoon of turmeric, the remaining ¼ teaspoon of paprika, the remaining ¼ teaspoon of black pepper, and the salt. Let simmer a minute or two, and then remove from the heat.
4. Equally divide the spinach mixture amongst the two naan breads. Place 1½ ounces of the marinated paneer on each naan.
5. Liberally spray the air fryer basket with olive oil mist.
6. Use a spatula to pick up one naan and place it in the air fryer basket.
7. Cook for 4 minutes, open the basket and sprinkle ¼ cup of mozzarella cheese on top, and cook another 4 minutes.
8. Remove from the air fryer and repeat with the remaining naan.
9. Serve warm.

Farfalle With White Sauce

Servings: 4 | Cooking Time: 30 Minutes

Ingredients:

- 4 cups cauliflower florets
- 1 medium onion, chopped
- 8 oz farfalle pasta
- 2 tbsp chives, minced
- ½ cup cashew pieces
- 1 tbsp nutritional yeast
- 2 large garlic cloves, peeled
- 2 tbsp fresh lemon juice
- Salt and pepper to taste

Directions:

1. Preheat air fryer to 390°F. Put the cauliflower in the fryer, spray with oil, and Bake for 8 minutes. Remove the basket, stir, and add the onion. Roast for 10 minutes or until the cauliflower is golden and the onions soft. Cook the farfalle pasta according to the package directions. Set aside. Put the roasted cauliflower and onions along with the cashews, 1 ½ of cups water, yeast, garlic, lemon, salt, and pepper in a blender. Blend until creamy. Pour a large portion of the sauce on top of the warm pasta and add the minced scallions. Serve.

Fried Rice With Curried Tofu

Servings:4 | Cooking Time: 25 Minutes

Ingredients:

- 8 oz extra-firm tofu, cubed
- ½ cup canned coconut milk
- 2 tsp red curry paste
- 2 cloves garlic, minced
- 1 tbsp avocado oil
- 1 tbsp coconut oil
- 2 cups cooked rice
- 1 tbsp turmeric powder
- Salt and pepper to taste
- 4 lime wedges
- ¼ cup chopped cilantro

Directions:

1. Preheat air fryer to 350ºF. Combine tofu, coconut milk, curry paste, garlic, and avocado oil in a bowl. Pour the mixture into a baking pan. Place the pan in the frying basket and Air Fry for 10 minutes, stirring once.
2. Melt the coconut oil in a skillet over medium heat. Add in rice, turmeric powder, salt, and black pepper, and cook for 2 minutes or until heated through. Divide the cooked rice between 4 medium bowls and top with tofu mixture and sauce. Top with cilantro and lime wedges to serve.

Vegan Buddha Bowls

Servings: 2 | Cooking Time: 45 Minutes

Ingredients:

- ½ cup quinoa
- 1 cup sweet potato cubes
- 12 oz broccoli florets
- ¾ cup bread crumbs
- ¼ cup chickpea flour
- ¼ cup hot sauce
- 16 oz super-firm tofu, cubed
- 1 tsp lemon juice

- 2 tsp olive oil
- Salt to taste
- 2 scallions, thinly sliced
- 1 tbsp sesame seeds

Directions:

1. Preheat air fryer to 400°F. Add quinoa and 1 cup of boiling water in a baking pan, cover it with aluminum foil, and Air Fry for 10 minutes. Set aside covered. Put the sweet potatoes in the basket and Air Fry for 2 minutes. Add in broccoli and Air Fry for 5 more minutes. Shake up and cook for another 3 minutes. Set the veggies aside.
2. On a plate, put the breadcrumbs. In a bowl, whisk chickpea flour and hot sauce. Toss in tofu cubes until coated and dip them in the breadcrumbs. Air Fry for 10 minutes until crispy. Share quinoa and fried veggies into 2 bowls. Top with crispy tofu and drizzle with lemon juice, olive oil and salt to taste. Scatter with scallions and sesame seeds before serving.

Powerful Jackfruit Fritters

Servings:4 | Cooking Time: 30 Minutes

Ingredients:

- 1 can jackfruit, chopped
- 1 egg, beaten
- 1 tbsp Dijon mustard
- 1 tbsp mayonnaise
- 1 tbsp prepared horseradish
- 2 tbsp grated yellow onion
- 2 tbsp chopped parsley
- 2 tbsp chopped nori
- 2 tbsp flour
- 1 tbsp Cajun seasoning
- ¼ tsp garlic powder
- ¼ tsp salt
- 2 lemon wedges

Directions:

1. In a bowl, combine jackfruit, egg, mustard, mayonnaise, horseradish, onion, parsley, nori, flour, Cajun seasoning, garlic, and salt. Let chill in the fridge for 15 minutes. Preheat air fryer to 350ºF. Divide the mixture into 12 balls. Place them in the frying basket and Air Fry for 10 minutes. Serve with lemon wedges.

Tortilla Pizza Margherita

Servings: 1 | Cooking Time: 15 Minutes

Ingredients:

- 1 flour tortilla
- ¼ cup tomato sauce
- 1/3 cup grated mozzarella
- 3 basil leaves

Directions:

1. Preheat air fryer to 350°F. Put the tortilla in the greased basket and pour the sauce in the center. Spread across the whole tortilla. Sprinkle with cheese and Bake for 8-10 minutes or until crisp. Remove carefully and top with basil leaves. Serve hot.

Spicy Sesame Tempeh Slaw With Peanut Dressing

Servings: 2 | Cooking Time: 8 Minutes

Ingredients:

- 2 cups hot water
- 1 teaspoon salt
- 8 ounces tempeh, sliced into 1-inch-long pieces
- 2 tablespoons low-sodium soy sauce
- 2 tablespoons rice vinegar
- 1 tablespoon filtered water
- 2 teaspoons sesame oil
- ½ teaspoon fresh ginger
- 1 clove garlic, minced
- ¼ teaspoon black pepper
- ½ jalapeño, sliced
- 4 cups cabbage slaw
- 4 tablespoons Peanut Dressing (see the following recipe)
- 2 tablespoons fresh chopped cilantro
- 2 tablespoons chopped peanuts

Directions:

1. Mix the hot water with the salt and pour over the tempeh in a glass bowl. Stir and cover with a towel for 10 minutes.
2. Discard the water and leave the tempeh in the bowl.
3. In a medium bowl, mix the soy sauce, rice vinegar, filtered water, sesame oil, ginger, garlic, pepper, and jalapeño. Pour over the tempeh and cover with a towel. Place in the refrigerator to marinate for at least 2 hours.
4. Preheat the air fryer to 370°F. Remove the tempeh from the bowl and discard the remaining marinade.
5. Liberally spray the metal trivet that goes into the air

fryer basket and place the tempeh on top of the trivet.
6. Cook for 4 minutes, flip, and cook another 4 minutes.
7. In a large bowl, mix the cabbage slaw with the Peanut Dressing and toss in the cilantro and chopped peanuts.
8. Portion onto 4 plates and place the cooked tempeh on top when cooking completes. Serve immediately.

Harissa Veggie Fries

Servings: 4 | Cooking Time: 55 Minutes

Ingredients:
- 1 pound red potatoes, cut into rounds
- 1 onion, diced
- 1 green bell pepper, diced
- 1 red bell pepper, diced
- 2 tbsp olive oil
- Salt and pepper to taste
- ¾ tsp garlic powder
- ¾ tsp harissa seasoning

Directions:

1. Combine all ingredients in a large bowl and mix until potatoes are well coated and seasoned. Preheat air fryer to 350°F. Pour all of the contents in the bowl into the frying basket. Bake for 35 minutes, shaking every 10 minutes, until golden brown and soft. Serve hot.

Kale & Lentils With Crispy Onions

Servings: 4 | Cooking Time: 40 Minutes

Ingredients:
- 2 cups cooked red lentils
- 1 onion, cut into rings
- ½ cup kale, steamed
- 3 garlic cloves, minced
- ½ lemon, juiced and zested
- 2 tsp cornstarch
- 1 tsp dried oregano
- Salt and pepper to taste

Directions:

1. Preheat air fryer to 390°F. Put the onion rings in the greased frying basket; do not overlap. Spray with oil and season with salt. Air Fry for 14-16 minutes, stirring twice until crispy and crunchy. Place the kale and lentils into a pan over medium heat and stir until heated through. Remove and add the garlic, lemon juice, cornstarch, salt, zest, oregano and black pepper. Stir well and pour in bowls. Top with the crisp onion rings and serve.

Mushroom Lasagna

Servings: 4 | Cooking Time: 40 Minutes

Ingredients:
- 2 tbsp olive oil
- 1 zucchini, diced
- ½ cup diced mushrooms
- ¼ cup diced onion
- 1 cup marinara sauce
- 1 cup ricotta cheese
- 1/3 cup grated Parmesan
- 1 egg
- 2 tsp Italian seasoning
- 2 tbsp fresh basil, chopped
- ½ tsp thyme
- 1 tbsp red pepper flakes
- ½ tsp salt
- 5 lasagna noodle sheets
- 1 cup grated mozzarella

Directions:

1. Heat the oil in a skillet over medium heat. Add zucchini, mushrooms, 1 tbsp of basil, thyme, red pepper flakes and onion and cook for 4 minutes until the veggies are tender. Toss in marinara sauce, and bring it to a bowl. Then, low the heat and simmer for 3 minutes.
2. Preheat air fryer at 375°F. Combine ricotta cheese, Parmesan cheese, egg, Italian seasoning, and salt in a bowl. Spoon ¼ of the veggie mixture into a cake pan. Add a layer of lasagna noodles on top, breaking apart noodles first to fit pan. Then, top with 1/3 of ricotta mixture and ¼ of mozzarella cheese. Repeat the layer 2 more times, finishing with mozzarella cheese on top. Cover cake pan with aluminum foil.
3. Place cake pan in the frying basket and Bake for 12 minutes. Remove the foil and cook for 3 more minutes. Let rest for 10 minutes before slicing. Serve immediately sprinkled with the remaining fresh basil.

General Tso's Cauliflower

Servings: 4 | Cooking Time: 15 Minutes

Ingredients:

- 1 head cauliflower cut into florets
- ¾ cup all-purpose flour, divided*
- 3 eggs, lightly beaten
- 1 cup panko breadcrumbs*
- canola or peanut oil, in a spray bottle
- 2 tablespoons oyster sauce
- ¼ cup soy sauce
- 2 teaspoons chili paste
- 2 tablespoons rice wine vinegar
- 2 tablespoons sugar
- ¼ cup water
- white or brown rice for serving
- steamed broccoli

Directions:

1. Set up dredging station using three bowls. Place the cauliflower in a large bowl and sprinkle ¼ cup of the flour over the top. Place the eggs in a second bowl and combine the panko breadcrumbs and remaining ½ cup flour in a third bowl. Toss the cauliflower in the flour to coat all the florets thoroughly. Dip the cauliflower florets in the eggs and finally toss them in the breadcrumbs to coat on all sides. Place the coated cauliflower florets on a baking sheet and spray generously with canola or peanut oil.
2. Preheat the air fryer to 400°F.
3. Air-fry the cauliflower at 400°F for 15 minutes, flipping the florets over for the last 3 minutes of the cooking process and spraying again with oil.
4. While the cauliflower is air-frying, make the General Tso Sauce. Combine the oyster sauce, soy sauce, chili paste, rice wine vinegar, sugar and water in a saucepan and bring the mixture to a boil on the stove top. Lower the heat and let it simmer for 10 minutes, stirring occasionally.
5. When the timer is up on the air fryer, transfer the cauliflower to a large bowl, pour the sauce over it all and toss to coat. Serve with white or brown rice and some steamed broccoli.

Italian-style Fried Cauliflower

Servings: 4 | Cooking Time: 35 Minutes

Ingredients:

- 2 eggs
- 1/3 cup all-purpose flour
- ½ tsp Italian seasoning
- ½ cup bread crumbs
- 1 tsp garlic powder
- 3 tsp grated Parmesan cheese
- Salt and pepper to taste
- 1 head cauliflower, cut into florets
- ½ tsp ground coriander

Directions:

1. Preheat air fryer to 370°F. Set out 3 small bowls. In the first, mix the flour with Italian seasoning. In the second, beat the eggs. In the third bowl, combine the crumbs, garlic, Parmesan, ground coriander, salt, and pepper.
2. Dip the cauliflower in the flour, then dredge in egg, and finally in the bread crumb mixture. Place a batch of cauliflower in the greased frying basket and spray with cooking oil. Bake for 10-12 minutes, shaking once until golden. Serve warm and enjoy!

Garlicky Roasted Mushrooms

Servings: 4 | Cooking Time: 30 Minutes

Ingredients:

- 16 garlic cloves, peeled
- 2 tsp olive oil
- 16 button mushrooms
- 2 tbsp fresh chives, snipped
- Salt and pepper to taste
- 1 tbsp white wine

Directions:

1. Preheat air fryer to 350°F. Coat the garlic with some olive oil in a baking pan, then Roast in the air fryer for 12 minutes. When done, take the pan out and stir in the mushrooms, salt, and pepper. Then add the remaining olive oil and white wine. Put the pan back into the fryer and Bake for 10-15 minutes until the mushrooms and garlic soften. Sprinkle with chives and serve warm.

Appendix : Recipes Index

"fried" Pickles With Homemade Ranch 26

A

Air-fried Potato Salad 76
Apple & Turkey Breakfast Sausages 19
Aromatic Mushroom Omelet 19
Avocado Toasts With Poached Eggs 14
Asian-style Shrimp Toast 21
Asian-style Salmon Fillets 71
Asparagus & Cherry Tomato Roast 74

B

Bbq Back Ribs 51
Black And Blue Clafoutis 40
Blackened Red Snapper 67
Blackened Catfish 65
Blossom Bbq Pork Chops 50
Breaded Avocado Tacos 88
Breakfast Frittata 14
Breakfast Chicken Sausages With Apples 16
Brownies After Dark 39
Buttermilk-fried Drumsticks 55
Butternut Squash–wrapped Halibut Fillets 71
Buttery Radish Wedges 75
Buttery Rolls 79
Baba Ghanouj 30
Banana Bread Cake 39
Banana Muffins With Chocolate Chips 11
Basic Chicken Breasts 56
Basic Chicken Breasts 61
Basic Corn On The Cob 79
Bengali Samosa With Mango Chutney 85
Beef Short Ribs 45

C

Chipotle Pork Meatballs 53
Charred Cauliflower Tacos 86
Cheddar-pimiento Strips 24
Cherry Hand Pies 36
Cheesy Egg Bites 18
Cheese & Honey Stuffed Figs 36
Cheese Blintzes 41
Cheese Arancini 26
Cheeseburger Slider Pockets 23
Cheese-rice Stuffed Bell Peppers 78
Chocolate Soufflés 33
Cinnamon Pumpkin Donuts 12
Cinnamon-stick Kofta Skewers 48
City "chicken" 50
Classic Stuffed Shells 77
Crispy Ham And Eggs 47
Crispy Avocados With Pico De Gallo 84
Crispy, Cheesy Leeks 82
Crunchy Fried Pork Loin Chops 52
Crunchy Parmesan Edamame 28
Crunchy Spicy Chickpeas 23
Creole Potato Wedges 75
Curried Potato, Cauliflower And Pea Turnovers 87
Curried Veggie Samosas 28
Cajun Fried Chicken 56
Cajun Chicken Livers 58
Calf's Liver 48
Cal-mex Turkey Patties 63
Calzones South Of The Border 46
Canadian Bacon & Cheese Sandwich 16
Caramel Apple Crumble 34
Catfish Nuggets 67
Catalan-style Crab Samfaina 65
Cauliflower "tater" Tots 29
Cauliflower 82
Corn & Shrimp Boil 68
Country-style Pork Ribs 48
Coconut Rice Cake 38
Coconut Shrimp With Plum Sauce 68

D

Dijon Chicken Wings 30
Dark Chocolate Cream Galette 37
Dauphinoise (potatoes Au Gratin) 77
Delicious Juicy Pork Meatballs 51

E

English Scones 17
Easy Bread Pudding 37
Easy Tex-mex Chimichangas 44
Easy Churros 32

F

Filled Mushrooms With Crab & Cheese 71
Fiery Chicken Meatballs 55
Fish Goujons With Tartar Sauce 71
Florentine Stuffed Tomatoes 81
Fried Banana S'mores 35
Fried Gyoza 25
Fried Pineapple Chunks 36
Fried Rice With Curried Tofu 90
Fried Eggplant Slices 74
Fried Scallops 66
Fried Oreos 41
Fried Corn On The Cob 80
French-style Steak Salad 53
Farfalle With White Sauce 90
Farmer´s Fried Chicken 63

G

Gingery Turkey Meatballs 59
Giant Buttery Oatmeal Cookie 34
Giant Buttery Chocolate Chip Cookie 40
Glazed Meatloaf 52
Grilled Ham & Muenster Cheese On Raisin Bread 28
Grilled Lime Scallions 79
Greek Pork Chops 48
Garlic Bread Knots 11
Garlic Parmesan Kale Chips 27
Garlic Wings 21
Garlic And Dill Salmon 70
Garlic-butter Lobster Tails 70
Garlic-herb Pita Chips 24
Garlicky Bell Pepper Mix 76
Garlicky Roasted Mushrooms 93
Garlic-cheese Biscuits 13
General Tso's Cauliflower 93
Gorgeous Jalapeño Poppers 84
Goat Cheese, Beet, And Kale Frittata 13

H

Huevos Rancheros 18
Halibut With Coleslaw 72
Harissa Veggie Fries 92
Healthy Granola 14
Healthy Chickpea Cookies 38
Home-style Fish Sticks 69
Honey-glazed Cornish Hen 59

I

Indian Fry Bread Tacos 45
Indian Chicken Tandoori 55
Irresistible Cheesy Chicken Sticks 58
Italian Roasted Chicken Thighs 57
Italian-inspired Chicken Pizzadillas 62
Italian-style Fried Cauliflower 93

J

Jalapeño Poppers 21
Jerk Chicken Drumsticks 57

K

Kielbasa Chunks With Pineapple & Peppers 51
Kale & Lentils With Crispy Onions 92
Kale Chips 22
Keto Cheesecake Cups 39

L

Lime Bay Scallops 70
Lemon Herb Whole Cornish Hen 56
Lemon Pound Cake Bites 42
Lemon Sage Roast Chicken 59
Lemon-garlic Strip Steak 47

Lentil Burritos With Cilantro Chutney 88

M

Middle Eastern Roasted Chickpeas 27
Mini Everything Bagels 11
Mini Carrot Cakes 35
Minted Lamb Chops 50
Mushroom & Quinoa-stuffed Pork Loins 45
Mushroom & Cavolo Nero Egg Muffins 13
Mushroom Lasagna 92
Mustard-crusted Rib-eye 49
Malaysian Shrimp With Sambal Mayo 69
Maple Balsamic Glazed Salmon 67
Mashed Potato Tots 77
Mexican Chicken Roll-ups 58
Mexican-style Salmon Stir-fry 66
Meat Loaves 53
Morning Chicken Frittata Cups 13
Moroccan-spiced Carrots 74
Moroccan-style Chicken Strips 57

N

Natchitoches Meat Pies 47

O

Old Bay Fish `n´ Chips 65
Orange Rolls 15
Orange-glazed Cinnamon Rolls 19
Oreo-coated Peanut Butter Cups 38
Oat Bran Muffins 15
Oatmeal Blackberry Crisp 33

P

Pizza Dough 12
Pizza Margherita With Spinach 86
Pickle Brined Fried Chicken 61
Parmesan Fish Bites 72
Parmesan Pizza Nuggets 25
Parmesan Eggplant Bites 22
Party Buffalo Chicken Drumettes 62
Party S´mores 32
Parsley Egg Scramble With Cottage Cheese 16
Patatas Bravas 81
Peppery Tilapia Roulade 69
Perfect Asparagus 77
Perfect Strip Steaks 46
Peanut Butter Cup Doughnut Holes 35
Peach Cobbler 42
Peachy Chicken Chunks With Cherries 58
Pecan-oat Filled Apples 40
Poblano Bake 59
Pork Tenderloin Salad 81
Pork Chops With Cereal Crust 49
Powerful Jackfruit Fritters 91

Q

Quinoa Burgers With Feta Cheese And Dill 88

R

Rib Eye Bites With Mushrooms 49
Rib Eye Cheesesteaks With Fried Onions 51
Rich Egg-fried Cauliflower Rice 23
Rich Salmon Burgers With Broccoli Slaw 70
Roasted Herbed Shiitake Mushrooms 80
Roasted Tomato And Cheddar Rolls 17

S

Shrimp Al Pesto 68
Simple Baked Potatoes With Dill Yogurt 75
Simple Salsa Chicken Thighs 62
Skirt Steak Fajitas 44
Spinach And Feta Stuffed Chicken Breasts 60
Spinach Cups 23
Spicy Sesame Tempeh Slaw With Peanut Dressing 91
Spicy Chicken And Pepper Jack Cheese Bites 22
Spring Vegetable Omelet 15
Spanish Fried Baby Squid 24
Speedy Shrimp Paella 65
Sticky Broccoli Florets 78
Sticky Drumsticks 56
Strawberry Donut Bites 37
Strawberry Donuts 33
Stuffed Prunes In Bacon 28
Sushi-style Deviled Eggs 84
Sweet Potato Fries 76
Sweet Potato Curly Fries 74
Sweet Corn Bread 84

Sage & Paprika Turkey Cutlets 56
Salmon Croquettes 69
Sardinas Fritas 68
Sea Scallops 72
Seared Scallops In Beurre Blanc 66
Seasoned Herbed Sourdough Croutons 18
Sesame-crusted Tuna Steaks 67
Southwest Cornbread 16
Southern Okra Chips 80
Scones 12

T

Thumbprint Sugar Cookies 32
Turkish Mutabal (eggplant Dip) 76
Turkey Bacon Dates 27
Turkey Tenderloin With A Lemon Touch 61
Two-cheese Grilled Sandwiches 86
Tandoori Paneer Naan Pizza 89
Tasty Brussels Sprouts With Guanciale 80
Tasty Roasted Black Olives & Tomatoes 26
Tempura Fried Veggies 29
Tomato & Halloumi Bruschetta 26
Tomato & Squash Stuffed Mushrooms 85
Tortilla Pizza Margherita 91
Tortilla Crusted Chicken Breast 60

V

Vietnamese Gingered Tofu 87
Veggie Burgers 86
Veggie Samosas 85
Vegan Buddha Bowls 90
Vegetable Couscous 89
Vegetarian Quinoa Cups 14

W

Whole-grain Cornbread 17

Z

Zucchini Fries 78
Za’atar Chicken Drumsticks 62
Zesty London Broil 49

Printed in Great Britain
by Amazon

21105079R00059